Interest and Inflation Free Money

Interest and Inflation Free Money

Creating an Exchange Medium
That Works for Everybody
and Protects the Earth

MARGRIT KENNEDY
WITH DECLAN KENNEDY
ILLUSTRATIONS BY
HELMUT CREUTZ

New Revised & Expanded Edition

NEW SOCIETY PUBLISHERS
PHILADELPHIA, PA • GABRIOLA ISLAND, BC

Library of Congress Cataloging-in-Publication Data:
Kennedy, Margrit I.
    Interest and inflation free money : creating an exchange medium that works for
everybody / Margrit Kennedy ; with Declan Kennedy.
       p.   cm.
    Includes bibliographical references and index.
    ISBN 0-86571-319-7
    1. Money. 2. Interest. 3. Inflation. 4. International finance. I. Kennedy,
Declan. II. Title.
HG221.K383 1995   332.4--dc20   95-10333

In the United States and Canada:	*Elsewhere in World:*
New Society Publishers	Seva International
4527 Springfield Avenue	2601 Cochise Lane
Philadelphia, PA 19143	Okemos, MI 48864

World hardcover and non-US or Canadian paperback versions published by Seva
International.

ISBN Paperback   USA 0-86571-319-7   CAN 1-55092-265-3

Typeset and designed by Sharp Designs of Holt, Michigan. Printed on partially-recycled
paper using soy-based ink by Capital City Press of Montpelier, Vermont.

To order directly from the publisher, add $3.00 to the price for the first copy, and add
75¢ for each additional copy. Send check or money order to:

In the United States:	*In Canada:*
New Society Publishers	New Society Publishers
4527 Springfield Avenue	PO Box 189
Philadelphia, PA 19143	Gabriola Island, BC V0R 1X0
(800) 333-9093	(800) 567-6772

New Society Publishers is a project of the New Society Educational Foundation, a
nonprofit, tax-exempt, public foundation in the United States, and of the Catalyst
Education Society, a nonprofit society in Canada. Opinions expressed in this book do
not necessarily represent positions of the New Society Educational Foundation, nor the
Catalyst Education Society.

Contents

List of Figures

Author's Acknowledgments

This book owes its existence to the many people in different parts of the world who were just as amazed to learn about the well-hidden fault in our present monetary system as I was when I first discovered it.

Their curiosity and enthusiasm about the analysis and the solution to the problem has led me to believe that the issue should be presented in a way which everybody can understand.

I want to thank especially three teachers: Helmut Creutz, Prof. Dr. Dicter Suhrt and Gesima Vogel. Further thanks to all responsible at Seva International, my new publisher, Shrikumar Poddar of Lansing, Michigan, U.S.A.

I extend my special thanks to my husband and co-author, Prof. Declan Kennedy, whose editorial, moral and practical support never failed to get me over the hurdles towards completion.

The illustrations are based on graphics researched and drawn by Helmut Creutz. Except for the figures relating to interest, all other statistics have been taken from publications of the West German Central Bank, the Federal Bureau of Statistics and other official documents before unification. The interest calculations have been derived from these figures.

Margrit Kennedy

PROF. DR. MARGRIT KENNEDY
Steyerberg, Germany
January 1995

Publisher's Note

During my trip to Australia in 1992 I was thrilled to discover Dr. Margrit Kennedy's book, *Interest and Inflation Free Money*.

For years I have been seeking solutions to the world's monetary ills and extreme concentration of wealth. This unique book gives us a revolutionary way to come out of the economic mess we are in all over the world.

I seek your help to make this book not only the best-selling economics book in the world but also to translate its ideas into practice.

Let us be partners in making this world peaceful, harmonious, just and environmentally sustainable.

Please buy this book in bulk for all your friends and family members as a wonderful gift.

Shrikumar Poddar

SHRIKUMAR PODDAR
Lansing, Michigan, U.S.A.
January 1995

Introduction

It takes some audacity for a non-economist to write a book about economics, especially if the book deals with one of the basic yardsticks of the profession, i.e., money. Money is the measure in which most economic concepts are expressed. Economists use it as merchants use kilograms and architects use metres. They seldom question the way it works and why in contrast to the meters and kilograms it is not a constant measure but varies, now, almost daily.

This book takes a look at how money works. It exposes the reason for the constant change in one of our most important measures. It explains why money not only "makes the world go round" but also wrecks the world in the process. The huge debt accumulated by Third World countries, unemployment, environmental degradation, the arms build-up and proliferation of nuclear power plants, are related to a mechanism which keeps money in circulation: interest and compound interest. This, according to economic historian John L. King, is the "invisible wrecking machine" in all so-called free-market economies.

Transforming this mechanism into a more adequate

way of keeping money in circulation is not as difficult as it may seem. While the solutions put forward in this book have been known to some people since the beginning of this century, the way and the time in which it is presented offer a special opportunity for its implementation.

The purpose of this book is not to prove anybody wrong. It is to put something right and to open up a choice we have which is hardly known among experts, not to mention the public at large. However, it is far too important to be left to experts alone to determine whether it will be dealt with or not. The significance of this book, therefore, lies in its ability to explain complex issues as simply as possible, so that everybody who uses money may understand what is at stake. Another significant difference from other books which have dealt with this issue in the past is that it shows how, at this particular point in time, the change to the proposed new monetary system could create a win-win situation for everyone. It could help to develop, finally, a sustainable economy.

The question remains whether we will be able to change before the next large breakdown happens or after it has happened. Either way it will be useful to be informed about how to create an exchange medium which works for everybody.

Four Basic Misconceptions
About Money

CHAPTER ONE

Four Basic Misconceptions About Money

EVERY DAY almost everyone on this planet uses money. Yet few people understand how money works and affects their lives directly and indirectly. Let us, therefore, take a closer look at what money is and what would happen without it.

First, the good news: Money is one of the most ingenious inventions of humankind, as it helps the exchange of goods and services and overcomes the limits of barter, that is, the direct exchange of goods and services. For example, if you live in a village which relies entirely on barter, and you produce works of art but there is nobody to exchange your artwork with except the undertaker, you will soon have to change your occupation or leave. Thus, money creates the possibility for specialization, which is the basis of civilization. Then why do we have a "money problem"?

Here comes the bad news: Money does not only help the exchange of goods and services but can also hinder the exchange of goods and services by being kept in the hands of those who have more than they need. Thus it creates a private toll gate where those who have less than they need pay a fee to those who have more money than they need. This is by no means a "fair deal." In fact, our present monetary systems could be termed "unconstitutional" in most democratic nations, as I will show later. Before going into more detail let me say that there are probably more than just four misconceptions about money. Our beliefs about money represent a fairly exact mirror of our beliefs about the world in which we live, and those are as varied as the number of people who live on this planet. However, the four misconceptions which will be discussed in the following pages are the most common hindrances to understanding why we must change the present money system and what mechanisms we need in order to replace it.

First Misconception
THERE IS ONLY ONE TYPE OF GROWTH

The first misconception relates to growth. We tend to believe that there is only one type of growth, that is, the growth pattern of nature which we have experienced ourselves. *Figure 1*, however, shows three generically different patterns:

Curve A represents an idealized form of the normal physical growth pattern in nature which our bodies follow, as well as those of plants and animals. We grow fairly quickly during the early stages of our lives, then begin to slow down in our teens, and usually stop growing physi-

Basic Types of Growth Patterns

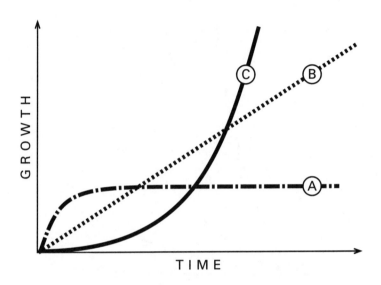

A. Natural curve
B. Linear curve
C. Exponential curve

FIGURE 1

Constant Growth Curves

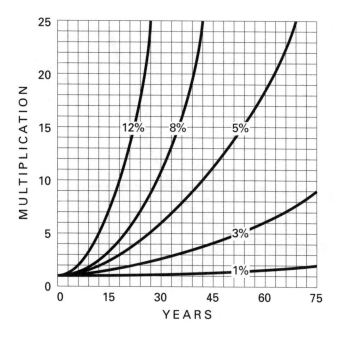

FIGURE 2

cally when we are about twenty-one. This, however, does not preclude us from growing further – "qualitatively" instead of "quantitatively."

Curve B represents a mechanical or *linear growth pattern*, e.g., more machines produce more goods, more coal produces more energy. It comes to an end when the machines are stopped, or no more coal is added.

Curve C represents an *exponential growth pattern* which may be described as the exact opposite to *curve A* in that it grows very slowly in the beginning, then continually faster, and finally in an almost vertical fashion. In the *physical* realm, this growth pattern usually occurs where there is sickness or death. Cancer, for instance, follows an exponential growth pattern. It grows slowly first, although always accelerating, and often by the time it has been discovered it has entered a growth phase where it cannot be stopped. Exponential growth in the *physical* realm usually ends with the death of the host and the organism on which it depends.

Based on interest and compound interest, our money doubles at regular intervals, i.e., it follows an exponential growth pattern. This explains why we are in trouble with our monetary system today. *Interest, in fact, acts like cancer in our social structure.*

Figure 2 shows the time periods needed for our money to double at compound interest rates:

■   at 3%, 24 years;
■   at 6%, 12 years;
■   at 12%, 6 years.

Even at 1% compound interest, we have an exponential growth curve, with a doubling time of 72 years.

Through our bodies we have only experienced the physical growth pattern of nature which stops at an optimal size (*Curve A*). Therefore, it is difficult for human beings to understand the full impact of the exponential growth pattern in the *physical* realm.

This phenomenon can best be demonstrated by the famous story of the Persian emperor who was so enchanted with a new chess game that he wanted to fulfill any wish the inventor of the game had. This clever mathematician decided to ask for one seed of grain on the first square of the chess board doubling the amounts on each of the following squares. The emperor, at first happy about such modesty, was soon to discover that the total yield of his entire empire would not be sufficient to fulfill the "modest" wish. The amount needed on the 64th square of the chess board equals 440 times the yield of grain of the entire planet.[1]

A similar analogy, directly related to our topic, is that one penny invested at the birth of Jesus Christ at 4% interest would have bought in 1750 one ball of gold equal to the weight of the earth. In 1990, however, it would buy 8,190 balls of gold. At 5% interest it would have bought one ball of gold by the year 1466. By 1990, it would buy 2,200 billion balls of gold equal to the weight of the earth.[2] The example shows the enormous difference 1% makes. *It also proves that the continual payment of interest and compound interest is arithmetically, as well as practically, impossible.* The economic necessity and the mathematical impossibility create a contradiction which – in order to be resolved – has led to innumerable feuds, wars and revolutions in the past.

Examples of the Amount of Interest Within Normal Prices & Fees

1. Garbage Collection Fees
    Example of the city of Aachen, 1983
    A. Depreciation, fixed, personnel
        and miscellaneous costs   88%
    B. *Cost of interest on capital*   *12%*
        Fees for a 110-litre garbage can: DM 194

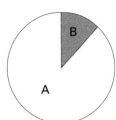

2. Drinking Water Costs
    Example of a northern German water supply works, 1981
    A. Energy costs   7%
    B. Plant maintenance   6%
    C. Water treatment   1%
    D. Personnel and fixed costs   18%
    E. Depreciation   30%
    F. *Cost of interest on capital*   *38%*
        Price per cubic metre: DM 136

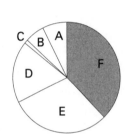

3. Use of Drains/Sewage Costs
    Example of the city of Aachen, 1983
    A. Fixed costs   19%
    B. Personnel costs   7%
    C. Depreciation   27%
    D. *Cost of interest on capital*   *47%*
        Price per cubic metre: DM 1.87

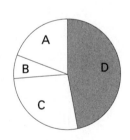

4. Cost of Rent in Public Housing
    Calculations of the Federal Office of Statistics, 1979
    A. Risk and profit   1%
    B. Administration and running costs   6%
    C. Building maintenance costs   5%
    D. Depreciation   11%
    E. *Cost of interest on capital*   *77%*
        Rent per square metre: DM 13.40

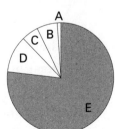

FIGURE 3

The solution to the problems caused by present exponential growth is to create a money system which follows the natural growth curve. That requires the replacement of interest by another mechanism to keep money in circulation. This will be discussed in detail in Chapter 2.

Second Misconception
WE PAY INTEREST ONLY
IF WE BORROW MONEY

A further reason why it is difficult for us to understand the full impact of the interest mechanism on our monetary system is that it works in a concealed way. Thus the second common misconception is that we pay interest only when we borrow money, and, if we want to avoid paying interest, all we need to do is avoid borrowing money.

Figure 3 shows that this is not true because interest is included in every price we pay. The exact amount varies according to the labor *versus* capital costs of the goods and services we buy. Some examples indicate the difference clearly. The capital share in garbage collection amounts to 12% because here the share of capital costs is relatively low and the share of physical labor is particularly high. This changes in the provision of drinking water, where capital costs amount to 38%, and even more so in social housing, where they add up to 77%. On an average we pay about 50% capital costs in the prices of our goods and services.

Therefore, if we could abolish interest and replace it with another mechanism to keep money in circulation, most of us could either be twice as rich or work half of the time to keep the same standard of living we have now.

Third Misconception
IN THE PRESENT MONETARY SYSTEM
WE ARE ALL EQUALLY AFFECTED BY INTEREST

A third misconception concerning our monetary system may be formulated as follows: Since everybody has to pay interest when borrowing money or buying goods and services, we are all equally well (or badly) off within our present monetary system.

Not true again. There are indeed huge differences as to who profits and who pays in this system. *Figure 4* shows a comparison of the interest payments and income from interest in ten numerically equal sections of the German population. It indicates that the first eight sections of the population pay more than they receive, the ninth section receives slightly more than it pays, and the tenth receives about twice as much interest as it pays, i.e., the tenth receives the interest which the first eight sections have lost. This explains graphically, in a very simple and straightforward way, why "the rich get richer and the poor get poorer."

If we take a more precise look at the last 10% of the population in terms of income from interest, another exponential growth pattern emerges. For the last 1% of the population the income column would have to be enlarged about 15 times. For the last 0.01% it would have to be enlarged more than 2,000 times.

In other words, within our monetary system we allow

Comparison of Interest Paid & Gained

In ten groups of households of 2.5 million each.

Applied interest paid or gained = DM 270 billion (1982)
(= interest transfer from private to private funds)

Applied credit interest = 5.5%

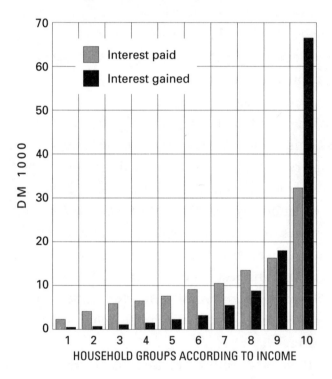

	1	2	3	4	5	6	7	8	9	10
Interest paid	2.3	4.1	5.9	6.5	7.6	9.1	10.5	13.5	16.3	32.3
Interest gained	0.5	0.7	1.1	1.5	2.3	3.2	5.5	8.8	18.0	66.5
Balance	−1.8	−3.4	−4.8	−5.0	−5.3	−5.9	−5.0	−4.7	+1.7	+34.2

All values in thousands of Deutche Marks per household per annum.

FIGURE 4

the operation of a hidden redistribution mechanism which constantly shuffles money from those who have less money than they need to those who have more money than they need. This is a different and far more subtle and effective form of exploitation than the one Marx tried to overcome. There is no question, that he was right in pointing to the source of the "added value" in the *production sphere*. The *distribution* of the "added value," however, happens to a large extent in the *circulation sphere*. This can be seen more clearly today than in his time. Ever larger amounts of money are concentrated in the hands of ever fewer individuals and corporations. For instance, the cash flow surplus, which refers to money floating around the world to wherever gains may be expected from changes in national currency or stock exchange rates, has more than doubled since 1980. The daily exchange of currencies in New York alone grew from $18 billion to $50 billion between 1980 and 1986.[3] The World Bank has estimated that money transactions on a world wide scale are from 15 to 20 times greater than necessary for financing world trade.[4]

The interest and compound interest mechanism not only creates an impetus for pathological economic growth but, as Dieter Suhr has pointed out, it works against the constitutional rights of the individual in most countries.[5] If a constitution guarantees equal access by every individual to government services – and the money system may be defined as such – then it is illegal to have a system in which 10% of the people continually receive more than they pay for that service at the expense of 80% of the people who receive less than they pay.

Development of Various Economic Indicators

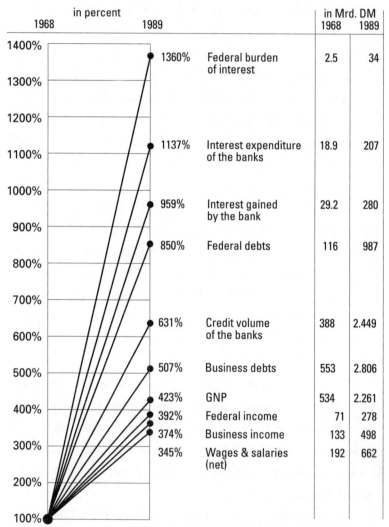

| in percent | | | | | in Mrd. DM | |
1968	1989				1968	1989
	1360%	Federal burden of interest			2.5	34
	1137%	Interest expenditure of the banks			18.9	207
	959%	Interest gained by the bank			29.2	280
	850%	Federal debts			116	987
	631%	Credit volume of the banks			388	2.449
	507%	Business debts			553	2.806
	423%	GNP			534	2.261
	392%	Federal income			71	278
	374%	Business income			133	498
	345%	Wages & salaries (net)			192	662

Source: Helmet Creutz from Reports of the Federal Bank, etc.

FIGURE 5

It may seem as if a change in our monetary system would serve "only" 80% of the population, i.e., those who at present pay more than their fair share. However, I will show in Chapter 3 that everybody profits from a cure, even those who profit from the cancerous system we have now.

Fourth Misconception
INFLATION IS AN INTEGRAL PART
OF FREE MARKET ECONOMIES

A fourth misconception relates to the role of inflation in our economic system. Most people see inflation as an integral part of any money system, almost "natural," since there is no capitalist country in the world with a free market economy without inflation. *Figure 5*, Development of Various Economic Indicators, shows some of the factors that may cause inflation. While the governmental income, the Gross National Product, and the salaries and wages of the average income earner "only" rose by about 400% between 1968 and 1989, the interest payments of the government rose by 1,360%.

The tendency is clear – government debts will sooner or later outgrow government income, even in the industrialized nations. If a child grew three times its size, say, between the ages of one and nine, but its feet grew to eleven times their size, we would call it sick. The problem here is that very few people care to see the signs of sickness in the monetary system, even fewer people know a remedy, and nobody has been able to set up a "healthy" working model which has lasted.

Few realize that inflation is just another form of taxation

BECAUSE OF INFLATION, EVERY DM IS WORTH ONLY 28 PFENNIGS

1950   1989

- What are the causes of this chronic fraud?
- Who wins and who loses?
- Why don't we have stable money?

FIGURE 6

through which governments can somewhat overcome the worst problems of increasing debt. Obviously, the larger the gap between income and debt, the higher the inflation needed. Allowing the central banks to print money enables governments to reduce debts. *Figure 6* shows the reduction of the value of the DM between 1950 and 1989. This devaluation hit that 80% of the people hardest who pay more most of time. They usually cannot withdraw their assets into "inflation-resistant" stocks, real estate or other investments like those who are in the highest 10% income bracket.

Economic historian, John L. King, links inflation to the interest paid for the "credit balloon." In a private letter to me, dated January 8, 1988, he states:

> I have written extensively about interest being the major cause of rising prices now since it is buried in the price of all that we buy, but this idea, though true, is not well accepted. $9 trillion in domestic U.S. debt, at 10% interest, is $900 billion paid in rising prices and this equates to the current 4% rise in prices experts perceive to be *inflation*. I have always believed the compounding of interest to be an invisible wrecking machine, and it is hard at work right now. So we must get rid of this mindless financial obsession.

A 1,000% expansion of private and public debt occurred in the U.S.A. during the last 33 years, the largest share coming from the private sector. But every resource of the Federal Government was utilized to spur this growth: loan guarantees, subsidized mortgage rates, low down-payments, easy terms, tax credits, secondary markets, deposit insurances, etc. The reason for this policy is that the only way to make the consequences of the interest system bearable for the large majority of the population is to create an economic growth which follows the exponential growth rate of money – a vicious circle with an accelerating, spiraling effect.

Whether we look at inflation, social equity, or environmental consequences, it would seem sensible from many points of view to replace the "mindless financial obsession" with a more adequate mechanism to keep money in circulation.

Creating an Interest and Inflation Free Money

CHAPTER TWO

Creating an Interest and Inflation Free Money

TOWARDS THE END of the 19th century Silvio Gesell, a successful merchant in Germany and Argentina, observed that sometimes his goods would sell quickly and yield a high price, and at other times slowly and attracted lower payments. He began to wonder why this was so. Soon he understood that these ups and downs had little to do with the needs of people for his goods, nor their quality, but almost exclusively with the "price" of money on the money market.

So he began to observe these movements and discovered that when interest rates were low, people would buy, but if they were high, they would not. The reason why there was sometimes more, sometimes less money, had to do with the willingness of the money owners to lend their money to others. If the return on their money was under 2.5%, they tended to hold on to their money – thus causing a halt in investment, with subsequent bankruptcies and decreasing numbers of jobs. Then after a while,

when people were ready to pay more interest for their
money, it would be available again – thus creating a new
economic cycle. There would be high interest rates and
high prices for goods at first, then gradually a larger supply
of money would create lower interest rates, and finally
there would be a "strike" of capital again.

Silvio Gesell's explanation for this phenomenon was
that money, unlike all other goods and services, can be
kept without costs. If one person has a bag of apples and
another person has the money to buy those apples, the
person with the apples is obliged to sell them within a
relatively short time period to avoid the loss of his assets.
Money owners, however, can wait until the price is right
for them; their money does not necessarily create "holding
costs."

Gesell concluded that if we could create a monetary
system which put money on equal footing with all other
goods and services, (charging, on the average, a 5% an-
nual maintenance cost, which is exactly what has been paid
in the form of interest for money throughout history) then
we could have an economy free of the ups and downs of
monetary speculation. He suggested that money should
be made to "rust," that is, to be subject to a "use fee."

REPLACEMENT OF INTEREST
BY A CIRCULATION FEE

In 1890, Silvio Gesell formulated a theory of money
and a "natural economic order"[6] which relates to capitalism or communism as the world of Copernicus does
to the world of Ptolemy. The sun indeed does not turn

around the earth; the earth turns around the sun – although our senses still defy this scientific truth. Gesell suggested securing the money flow by making money a government service subject to a use fee. And this is the central message of this book. *Instead of paying interest to those who have more money than they need and in order to keep money in circulation, people should pay a small fee if they keep the money out of circulation.*

In order to understand this idea better, it is helpful to compare money to a railroad freight car which also helps to facilitate the exchange of goods and services. In contrast to governments which issue money, however, the railroad company does not pay the user a premium to unload the freight car and thereby bring it back into "circulation" – instead the user pays a small *per diem* fee if he or she does not unload it. This is all we would have to do with money. The community or nation which issues "new" money in order to help the exchange of goods and services charges a small "parking" fee to the user who holds on to new money longer than he or she needs for exchange purposes. This change, simple as it may seem, resolves the many societal problems caused by interest and compound interest throughout history.

While interest nowadays is a private gain, the fee on the use of money would be a public gain. This fee would have to return into circulation in order to maintain the balance between the volume of money and the volume of economic activities. The fee would serve as an income to the government, and thereby reduce the amount of taxes needed to carry out public tasks.

The technical side of this monetary reform will be explained in the next two sections.

THE FIRST MODEL EXPERIMENTS

During the 1930s, the *Freiwirtschaft* (free economy) followers of Gesell's theory found opportunities to initiate interest-free money projects, in order to overcome unemployment and to demonstrate the validity of their ideas. There were endeavours to introduce free-money in Austria, France, Germany, Spain, Switzerland, and the United States. One of the most successful was in the town of Wörgl in Austria.[7]

Between 1932 and 1933, the small Austrian town of Wörgl started an experiment which has been an inspiration to all who have been concerned with the issue of monetary reform up to this day. The town's mayor convinced the business people and administrators that they had a lot to gain and nothing to lose if they conducted a monetary experiment in the way suggested in Silvio Gesell's book *The Natural Economic Order.*

People agreed and so the town council issued 32,000 "Work Certificates" or "Free Schillings" (i.e., interest-free Schillings), covered by the same amount of ordinary Austrian Schillings in the bank. They built bridges, improved roads and public services, and paid salaries and materials with this money, which was accepted by the butcher, the shoemaker, the baker.

The fee on the use of the money was 1% per month or 12% per year. This fee had to be paid by the person who had the banknote at the end of the month, in the form of a stamp worth 1% of the note and glued to its back. Otherwise, the note was invalid. This small fee caused everyone who got paid in Free Schillings to spend them before they used their ordinary money. People even paid their taxes in advance in order to avoid paying the small fee. Within one year, the 32,000 Free Schillings circulated 463 times, thus creating goods and services worth over 14,816,000 Schillings. The ordinary Schilling by contrast circulated only 21 times.[8]

At a time when most countries in Europe had severe problems with decreasing numbers of jobs, Wörgl reduced its unemployment rate by 25% within this one year. The fees collected by the town government which caused the money to change hands so quickly amounted to a total of 12% of 32,000 Free Schillings = 3,840 Schillings. This was used for public purposes.

When over 300 communities in Austria began to be interested in adopting this model, the Austrian National Bank saw its own monopoly endangered. It intervened against the town council and prohibited the printing of its local money. In spite of a long-lasting battle which went right up to the Austrian Supreme Court, neither Wörgl nor any other community in Europe has been able to repeat the experiment up to the present day.

In his book *Capitalism at its Best*,[9] Dieter Suhr presents a report on the U.S. "stamp scrip movement" by Hans R. L. Cohrssen who, together with economist, Irving Fisher, tried to introduce Gesell's concept of cost-bearing money into the U.S.A. – also in 1933. At that time, more than 100 communities, including several large cities, had planned to implement *stamp scrip money*. The issue

went right up to the Secretary of Labor, the Secretary of
the Interior and the Secretary of the Treasury in Washington, D.C., none of whom were opposed – but none
of whom had the power to grant the necessary permis-
sions. Finally, Dean Acheson (who later became Secretary of State) asked for an opinion from the government's
economic advisor, Harvard Professor Russell Sprague, before he could make a decision. Cohrssen remembers the
meeting as a very cordial one:

> Professor Sprague told me … that in principle there was
> nothing to be said against the issue of stamp scrip for the
> purpose of creating jobs. However, our scheme went much
> further: It was an attempt to restructure the American mon-
> etary system and he had no authority to approve such a pro-
> posal. That put an end not only to our stamp scrip movement
> but to a model project that might indeed have led to mon-
> etary reform.[10]

On March 4, 1933, President Roosevelt directed the
banks to be temporarily closed, and he forbade any further issue of emergency currency. Cohrssen concludes:

> In summary we can say that the technical difficulties of
> attaining currency stability seem minor in comparison to the
> general lack of understanding of the problem itself. As long
> as the *Money Illusion* … is not overcome it will be virtually
> impossible to muster the political will power necessary for
> this stability.[11]

According to Otani's proposal,[12] the technical side of
the reform, based on the payment modes of today, would
make a "use-fee" on the new money a much simpler issue. Ninety percent of what we call "money" are num-

bers in a computer. Thus, everyone would have two accounts: one checking account (in Europe this is called a current account, in Australia an access account) and one savings account. The money in the checking account, which is at the disposal of the owner continually, would be treated like cash and might lose as little as ½% per month or 6% per year. Anyone with more new money in her or his checking account than needed for the payment of all expenses in a particular month, would be prompted by the small fee to transfer that amount to a savings account. From there, the bank would be able to lend this money without interest to those who needed it, for a certain amount of time, and, therefore, the savings account would *not* be debited with a fee (*see Chapter 6*).

By the same token, the new money owner would not receive any interest on his or her savings account – *but the new money would retain its value.* As soon as interest is abolished, inflation becomes unnecessary (*see Chapter 1*). The person receiving a credit would not pay interest, but risk premium and bank charges quite comparable to those which are included in every bank loan. This amounts in Germany today to about 2.5% of the normal credit costs.

Thus very little would change in practice. Banks would operate as usual, except that they would be more interested in giving loans because they too would be subject to the same use fee that everybody else would have to pay. In order to balance the amount of credit and savings available temporarily, banks might have to pay or receive a small amount of interest depending on whether or not they had more new money in saving accounts than they needed or whether they had liquidity problems. In this case the interest would only serve as a regulatory mechanism and not as a wealth redistribution mechanism as it does today.

The basis of this reform would be a fairly accurate adaptation of the amount of money in circulation to the amount of money needed to handle all transactions. When enough new money has been created to serve all transactions, no more would have to be produced. That means new money would now follow a "natural" physical growth pattern (*curve A, Figure 1*) and no longer an exponential growth pattern.

Another technical aspect of the implementation of such a monetary reform includes the prevention of hoarding cash. A more elegant solution than gluing a stamp on the back of a banknote would be the printing of different coloured banknotes so that various series could be recalled once or twice a year, without prior announcement. This would be no more expensive for the government of a country than the replacement of old worn-out banknotes by new ones as happens today.

As the Austrian and American experiences show, the political side is more crucial than the technical. It will be dealt with in Chapter 3.

If the above-described monetary reform were to be implemented on a large scale, an accompanying land tax reform would be required. Without land reform there would be a tendency for surplus money to be attracted to land speculation. Without tax reform, the economic boom following the introduction of interest free money might have some serious environmental consequences.

THE NEED FOR LAND REFORM

Money and land are two things everybody needs in order to live. Whether we eat, sleep or work, life is impossible without land. Land, like air and water, therefore, should belong to everybody. The North American Indians say "The Earth is our Mother. How could we divide her up and sell her?" *Land should belong to the community and then be rented out by the community to those who use it.* This was the concept and the custom in many European countries until the introduction of Roman law in the Middle Ages with its emphasis on private property.

Today, the world is split into two systems:

- private ownership and private use of land in the capitalist countries;
- communal ownership and communal use of land in the communist countries.

In capitalist countries, the majority of the people pay for the huge profits from speculation in private land (*Figure 7*), and more land is concentrated in the hands of ever fewer people. In communist countries, the uneconomic use of communal land is the major problem. In former West Germany about 70% of the land belonged to 20% of the people. In Brazil and other Third World countries, the land-owning minority is often as small as 2–3% of the population. The problem in capitalist countries, therefore, has to do with private ownership of land.

In communist countries, in the former Soviet Union, for example, where land was communally owned and used, about 60% of the food was being produced on that 4% of the land which was owned privately. This meant that

To Pay for a Building Site in the F.R.G. in the 1980s, People Had to Work Three Times as Much as in the 1950s

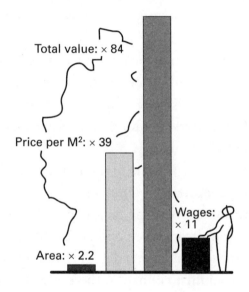

Without considering the contribution of the owners, the value of building sites increased by DM 1 trillion since 1950.

- Why does land become more and more expensive to buy?
- Who are the beneficiaries of the present policy?
- What would have to change to create more equity?

FIGURE 7

the problem here was communal ownership and use.

A combination of *private use* and *communal ownership* would be the most advantageous solution for achieving social justice and allowing individual growth. This is what was suggested by Henry George in 1879,[13] Silvio Gesell in 1904,[14] and Yoshito Otani in 1981.[15]

In practical terms today, it would mean that a community would buy up all its land and lease it out to its inhabitants. Countries with a progressive constitution would have no trouble implementing this change from an ideal point of view. Thus the constitution of the former Federal Republic of Germany described land as an asset which carries a "social" responsibility. Up to this date, however, this social responsibility has not been met. *Figure 7* shows that, on the average, people had to work three times as long in 1982 as they did in 1950 in order to pay for a piece of property.

After the catastrophic results of expropriation in countries with a communist constitution, no western nation today would be able to discuss the dispossession of land by the state without compensation. Although Roman law, which introduced private ownership of land into western civilization (roughly 500 years ago), was forced on the people by their conquerors, those who profited – at first – belong to history, and today's owners have either bought or inherited quite legally the soil they occupy. Therefore, some compensation must be paid if a society wants to create a more equitable situation.

One long-term possibility is to levy a small fee of about 3% per year on the value of each plot of land. This fee would be paid to the community and would be used to buy land which came on the market. Thus the community would acquire the ownership of its land in a little over 33 years.

An alternative would be that land owners would be notified that they had the option not to pay the fee but to sell their land to the community. For instance, the 3% fee would be set off against the normal price over 33 years. No money would be exchanged. Meanwhile the owners still would have the right to use the land – but after the 33 years they would have to pay a 3% lease on the value of the land annually to the community.

The immediate effect of this regulation would be to stop land speculation. Most land which people hold today without using it would be offered on the market in order to avoid a continual loss. As more land became available, the price of land would fall and more people would have a chance to use the available land in a productive manner. Mainly in developing countries, this could have a considerable effect on food production, as the diminishing ratio of food in comparison to the amount of people to be fed is not a question of agricultural technique, but a question of the availability of land for small scale farms.

Whether in developing or industrialized countries, the tenants would have all the advantages of today's hereditary leasehold regulations in this new system. They could use their property within the confines of local planning restrictions. They could build on it. They could sell their houses. They could bequeath their houses to their descendants. They could let them out to third parties without involving the community as long as the next tenants would pay the lease. By determining the exact amount of the rent through public bids, auctions or similar processes, the inefficiency of the planned economy or bureaucratic procedures could be avoided.

This change would, at long last, take an enormous load off the shoulders of the working population who, in the end, always pay for every profit based on speculation. The latter, indeed, is what land has always been used for. A realistic change towards a social solution, therefore, must eliminate speculation with land and money. Again, the proposed solution does not aim at punishing those who profit from the present system, but it is designed to put an end, slowly but surely, to the preconditions which allow enormous advantages to a few people while requiring the large majority to pay for them.

THE NEED FOR TAX REFORM

In Germany today it has been estimated that between one-half to two-thirds of the Gross National Product may be termed "questionable" in respect to maintaining an ecologically sustainable future.[16] Therefore, removing the barriers to initiate more production and employment through the proposed money and land reforms may require two changes in the way taxes are levied, or else environmental devastation would likely increase:

(1) a change from an income tax to a product tax;
(2) an assessment of the costs to the environment included in this product tax.

Hermann Laistner,[17] who explains this idea in detail in his book *Die Ökologische Wirtschaft* (*The Ecological Economy*), points out that income taxes eventually make labor more expensive and, therefore, makes more mechanization necessary. This encourages the consumption of finite resources through increasingly cheap consumer products. If a tax on products would be introduced, instead, which also would include the costs of the product to the environment, products would tend to become relatively more expensive. Combined with lower labor costs, this would reduce the pressure for more automation and more people could find employment.

Right now, society pays twice if a laborer is replaced by a machine. It loses the income tax – as incomes of machines are not taxed – and subsequently pays unemployment benefits to the laid-off laborer. In addition, a sizable portion of work is carried out illegally at present, in order to avoid income taxes. If income tax were abolished, this shadow economy would finally become legal.

While not causing any lowering of the standard of living to start with, because the increase in prices for products would be balanced by a tax-free income, this change would create very different and more ecologically-sound consumer behaviour in the long run. People would think twice before they got a new bicycle or car if it were a lot more expensive than to repair the old one.

The change in taxation could be introduced gradually and would make sense even without the monetary and land reforms. It would support effectively a large number of demands and proposals from ecologists during the last decades. Combined with the two other reforms, this change would render redundant many environmental issues and "protection measures" while contributing to solving unemployment problems.

Who Would Profit from a
New Monetary System?

Who Would Profit from a New Monetary System?

INDIVIDUAL AND SOCIAL CHANGE seems to happen for three basically different reasons:

(1) because a breakdown due to a particular pattern of behaviour *has* occurred, i.e., in order to avoid another occurrence;

(2) because a breakdown due to a particular pattern of behaviour *may* occur, i.e., in order to avoid the break-down;

(3) because another pattern of behaviour *seems more adequate* in order to achieve the desired result.

The change in the monetary system proposed in the last chapter may happen for any one, any combination, or all of the above reasons:

(1) In the past, the cancerous accumulation of wealth has been dissolved regularly by social revolutions, wars and economic collapse. The unprecedented economic interdependency of all nations today and the multifold potential for global destruction ren-

ders this kind of conflict resolution mechanism unacceptable. We are forced to search for new solutions to avoid another war, social revolution or economic collapse.

(2) According to many specialists in the field of economics and banking the 1987 stock market crash in which $1.5 trillion vanished within a few days was only a small ripple compared to the imminent danger of a worldwide second Great Depression, which is likely to happen if we don't introduce fundamental change within the next few years.[18] Changing the monetary system now offers one possibility for avoiding the enormous human and material costs of such a disaster.

(3) Whether or not we can see that every exponential growth curve eventually leads to its own destruction, the advantages of the change to a new monetary system are so evident in terms of social and environmental equity that this path should be chosen simply because it is a better one than what we have at present.

However, the main problem in any transformation process is not so much that we want to stay where we are or that we don't see the advantages of where we want to be. It is more: How do we get from here to there, from this trapeze to the one over there, without endangering our lives?

In order to make it easier to see how this transformation could assist in reaching the goals of many very different social groups, let us take a closer look first at the flaws in the monetary system and then at the advantages of a new monetary system for the rich and the poor, governments and individuals, minorities and the majority, industrialists and environmentalists, materially oriented people and spiritually oriented people. The interesting fact which emerges is that, at this particular point in time, in this crisis situation which we have created for ourselves, *everybody* would be better off with a new monetary system. We all are in a win-win situation if we implement the necessary change. But we need to do it soon.

THE ADVANTAGES IN GENERAL

Up to this point of the analysis we have dealt with facts and figures which anyone can verify. From now on we are dealing with "educated guesses," based on experiences in the past. The accuracy of these predictive guesses will have to be validated by real-life examples.

The question, therefore, arises: why would any region or country opt for trying out, and serving as a testing ground, for a new monetary system?

If our analysis has been correct so far, then the proposed solution offers among other things the following main benefits:

(1) the elimination of inflation;
(2) the increase of social equity;
(3) decreasing unemployment;
(4) the lowering of prices by 30–50%;
(5) an initial economic boom;
(6) and thereafter a stable economy.

FLAWS IN THE MONETARY SYSTEM

In most countries, the monopoly to print money rests in the hands of the central government. Any trial run of the new money system, therefore – even on a smaller regional scale – would have to be supported by the government. Obviously the introduction of an interest-free money would be a highly political issue. It takes courage for any government to admit that a system of such inequity has been tolerated so far. On the other hand, it is clearly very difficult for most people to see why a "fee" on money is a better solution than interest.

At present government leaders, politicians, bankers and economists try to respond to the problems which are caused by the basic flaws in the monetary system by treating symptoms and offering band-aid solutions. In election campaigns there are regular promises to combat inflation, to improve social services and to support environmental concerns and conservation issues.

The truth of the matter is that they are fighting with their backs to the wall, and that the situation is not improving but rather deteriorating, as we come closer to the acceleration phase of the exponential growth curve of the monetary system. Instead of improvements in the social and environmental sectors, budget cuts force a deterioration. Whether politicians belong to the conservative or progressive wing, the room for real change in the present system is small indeed.

Figure 8 implies why this happens. In any highly diversified economy one sector is intimately connected with another. If we take away more than its share from one

WHY DOES THE ECONOMY GET CAUGHT IN THE COGS?

- Can this chain of reactions be broken?
- Who would have to intervene?
- What would have to be changed in the circulation mechanism?

FIGURE 8

sector, we are bound to cause trouble – not only there –
but also in others. If government debts and interest rise,
more money flows to the owners of monetary wealth. At
the same time, those who work have less money to con-
sume. This, in turn, causes market fluctuations with in-
fluences on employment opportunities. Governments
which increase debts in order to close gaps in their income invariably increase the "problem chain." The new
money system would help to reduce the disproportionate rise in debts as well as the concentration of money-
wealth and would secure the steady exchange of goods and
services on a free market.

If we think that the situation seems difficult in industrialized countries, we must look at Third world countries which carry the worst consequences of the present-day
system. While large American and German banks are increasing their reserves to be prepared for the fiscal break-
downs of their debtors in industrially developing countries,
industrialized countries continue to import capital from
developing countries. By exporting new loans to help pay
off old ones, they prolong and magnify the international
debt crisis. That this trend must change has been shown
clearly in the report of the UN World Commission on
Environment and Development entitled "Our Common
Future." It also proves that the seemingly separate crises
of the world's economy and the planet's ecology are, in
fact, one.

> Ecology and economy are becoming ever more interwoven
> – locally, regionally, nationally, and globally – into a seam-
> less net of causes and effects ... Debts that they cannot pay
> force African nations relying on commodity sales to over-

use their fragile soils, thus turning land to desert ...

The production base of other developing world areas suffers similarly both from local failures and from the workings of international economic systems. As a consequence of the 'debt crisis' of Latin America, that region's natural resources are now being used not for development but to meet financial obligations to creditors abroad.

This approach to the debt problem is short-sighted from several standpoints: namely, economic, political, and environmental. It requires relatively poor countries simultaneously to accept growing poverty while exporting growing amounts of scarce resources.

Inequality is the planet's main 'environmental' problem; it is also its main 'development' "problem."[20]

By now according to Mr. Herrhaus, manager of the largest German bank (Deutsche Bank): "the structure and dimension of the problem defies traditional problem- solving techniques."[21]

Those who operate the present money system know that it cannot last, but either do not know or do not want to know about a practical alternative. *Figure 9* gives at least one explanation. Compared to the Gross National Product and the increase in debt, the banks have earned a disproportionate share of the national wealth. This is in part connected with lower interest rates which offer better profits for banks, but also to the increased speculation with money, leading to an increase in brokerage fees. The bankers with whom I have discussed this issue did not know of the alternative. After I explained it, they often felt that they could not pass the knowledge on without endangering their jobs.

Banks are not interested in an open discussion of how

GROWTH OF THE GNP IN THE F.R.G.
BETWEEN 1950 AND 1989

The GNP grew 22 times

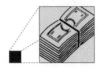

The national debt grew 75 times

Bank transactions grew 88 times

- Where does the overgrowth in the monetary sector originate?
- What are the consequences for society?
- What could be done to reduce the imbalance?

FIGURE 9

the interest system works, unless they take a long- term view. At present, they behave rather to the contrary. *Figure 10* demonstrates some misleading headlines which can be found in advertisements of banks in magazines and news- papers all over the world. Money – banks say – should "grow," "increase," "multiply." Most often, they try to impress people with the idea that money should "work" for them. However, nobody has ever seen money work- ing. Work has always been done by people with or with- out machines.

These advertisements conceal the fact that every DM or dollar which goes to the investor of money is the ac- complishment of another person from whom this amount is being taken away, no matter in which way that might happen. In other words, people who work for their money are getting poorer at the same rate at which the invest- ment of those who own money doubles. That is the whole mystery of how money "works," which banks do not like to have uncovered.

In my experience, those who should be aware of the problem and the solution through their education, i.e., economists are afraid of being branded as "radicals." In- deed, by supporting interest-free money, they would be trying to get at the root (in Latin = *radix*) of one of the world's most pressing economic problems.

Two of the great personalities of this century, Albert Einstein and John Maynard Keynes clearly saw the im- portance of Gesell's monetary reform ideas. Keynes ac- tually stated in 1936 that "the future would learn more from the spirit of Gesell than from Marx."[22]

This future, however, has not started as yet; although

HAVE YOU EVER SEEN MONEY WORK?

MONEY HAS TO WORK ...

for good
dividends!

Make more money
out of your money.

If you make your money work right,
you can retire without worry.

You can make
more out of
this Mark.

MONEY

makes money

makes money

makes money

DM 200,000, on an average, work
at every place of employment.

- How can you make more money out of money?
- Who contributes to productivity?
- Who benefits when money "works"?

FIGURE 10

bankers and economists do not need to be terribly far-sighted to recognize that a new money system would enable them to resolve the central dilemma which they have been wrestling with for decades. Instead, as economic historian John L. King states in his book *On the Brink of the Great Depression II*:

> Their number-crunching and computerized formulas have proven to be wildly irrelevant and thus their predictions have become famously wrong. It's as though we have educated these people beyond their capacities to think.[23]

My observation is, that in contrast to most engineers, economists do not really understand the danger incurred in exponential growth. They may recognize its danger in the proliferation of AIDS or in the "population explosion." In their own field, however, they seem almost blind, and naively confident that symptomatic treatment, here and there, will prove sufficient to slow down the danger.

Governments introducing monetary reform soon would go a long way towards securing social equity, ecological survival and curing the money diseases which have plagued the so-called "free market economies" for decades.

ADVANTAGES FOR THE REGION OR COUNTRY WHICH INTRODUCES THESE CHANGES FIRST

The possibility to invest and produce without having to pay interest would not only lower the prices for these goods and services in the regions or countries which introduce the new money system, but also create an enormous advantage for industries and products competing on the national or world market. Whatever the going interest rate, products and services could be sold that much cheaper. This would result in a fast economic boom in the regions introducing interest-free money first.

A disadvantage could be seen in this change as being a threat to the environment. However, apart from the possibility of creating a better system of taxation (as described above), we might look at the following possibility.

Many products and services which at present cannot compete with the money-making power of money on the money market would suddenly become economically feasible. Among these would be many ecological products, social projects and artistic endeavours which often would be carried out if they could just "break even." This would result in a more diversified and stable economic base, which is anything but threatening to the environment.

Unemployment rates would drop when economic activities blossom, decreasing the need for social security payments, ever larger bureaucracies and higher taxes.

If introduced in a *particular region*, there would have to be an automatic low cost exchange rate to facilitate trade between this region and other regions in the country. Until the whole country would adopt the new money system, certain regulations might have to be established to prevent speculative exchange deals.

If introduced in a *whole country*, trading with foreign countries would continue as it does today. There would still be an ordinary exchange rate. Comparatively speaking, however, the "stable money" would attract higher exchange rates over the years in comparison with other currencies, because it would not be subject to devaluation through inflation. Therefore, investments in this money could be quite advantageous in comparison with fluctuating currencies such as the dollar at present.

As in the case of Wörgl described previously *(see Chapter 2)* – it would be possible even for two monetary systems to exist side by side. We could keep the one we have at present and introduce the new money, even in a smaller region or town. According to Gresham's Law, "bad" money displaces "good" money. What we are newly creating here is – in his sense – "bad" money – money which is subject to a use fee unlike the present money. Wherever people can pay with the "bad" money, they will pass it on – and they will hold on to the "good" money. Thus the new money will be used wherever possible, which is exactly what we want. The old money will be kept and used to the extent necessary. Therefore, introduced as an experiment in a specific region in the beginning, the proposed money system could also co-exist with our present system until it had proven its usefulness. Who else would benefit from a new monetary system?

THE RICH

One of the critical questions which is always asked by people who begin to understand the effectiveness of the hidden redistribution mechanism in our present money system is: Will those 10% of the population who profit from this mechanism at present allow any change which might eliminate their chances to extract a work-free income from the large majority of people?

The historic answer is: Of course not, unless they are forced by those who pay. The new answer is: Of course they will, if they become aware of the fact that "the branch on which they are sitting grows on a sick tree" and that there is a "healthy alternative tree" which is not going to collapse sooner or later. The second means social evolution, the soft path. The first means social revolution, the hard path.

The soft path offers rich people the chance of keeping the money they have gained through interest. The hard path will invariably lead to sizable losses.

The soft path means no accusation because of profits from interest, until we introduce the new money system, since their behaviour has been totally within their legal rights. The hard path of social revolution may well be more painful.

The soft path means no more interest earning money but a stable currency, lower prices and, possibly, lower taxes. The hard path means growing insecurity, instability, higher inflation, higher prices, and higher taxes.

So far my experience with people in the "richest 10% category" has been that they are neither fully aware of how the interest system really operates, nor that there are any practical alternatives. With few exceptions, they would tend to opt for security rather than more money, since they mostly have enough for themselves and sometimes for many generations to come.

The second question is: What happens if the rich transfer their money to other countries where they get interest, instead of putting it into their savings account where it retains its value but it does not accumulate interest?

The answer is that within a very short period after the introduction of the reform, they may do just the opposite. Because the margin of profit between what people gain in other countries from interest after they deduct inflation would most likely be about the same as the increase in value of the new money in their own country which is not subject to inflation.

In fact, the danger may be precisely the other way around. What we may create is a "Super-Switzerland" with a stable currency and a booming economy. For several years in Switzerland, investors even had to pay interest in order to leave their money in a bank account. In contrast, the U.S.A. offered the highest interest rates in the early Reagan era and attracted surplus money from all over the world and soon had to devalue the dollar drastically in order to meet its obligations to creditors abroad. At 15% interest, the U.S.A. would have had to repay about twice the amount invested by foreign lenders after 5 years. There was no way in which this could have been achieved had the dollar been kept at its original value. One further consequence of this policy was that the U.S.A. changed from being the largest creditor to being the largest debtor nation in the world within a time span of only eight years.

The huge amount of speculative money which is estimated to be as high as $50 billion – circulating the world from one banking center to the next in search of profitable investment – shows that there is a shortage of sensible investment opportunities rather than a shortage of money. This would change, in any region or country, which by introducing interest-free money created a booming, and finally stable and diversified economy. Chances are that surplus money from outside would be invested here rather than that surplus money from inside would leave the region.

In many ways, it would be more profitable for rich people to help monetary reform to happen and to support a stable system rather than to support growing instability and risk the inevitable crash.

A third question concerning the richest 10% of the population relates to those who live on their capital and are too old to work. What happens to them if interest is abolished?

An example taken from Germany (in terms of average interest and inflation rates) shows that those who can live off their interest now can live off their capital at least for one, if not for two or more, generations. If we assume capital assets of 1,000,000 DMarks, an average interest rate of 7% and an average rate of inflation of 3%, the gross income amounts to 40,000 DMarks per year, without depleting the capital.

In the new money system we abolish interest and inflation, thereby reducing the prices of all goods and services as well as taxes by about 40%. This means that this person needs a gross income of 24,000 DMarks per year in order to keep the same standard of living as in the present system. If we divide 1,000,000 by 24,000, we see that this person could live for 40 years off her or his capital.

The point of this example is that almost anybody who can at present live off their own capital will also be able to live off their capital if we change the monetary system.

Among the richest 10% of the population in terms of wealth are those with assets over one million DMarks. But there are some who gain more than one million DMarks from their interest every day. According to official sources,[24] the daily income of the Queen of England, the richest woman in the world, was 700,000 pounds (roughly two million DMarks) in 1982. Although neither the Queen nor firms like Siemens, Daimler-Benz and General Motors have much official power, their ownership of money is, in fact, unofficial power. Scandals concerning the pay-offs by leading industries financing political parties in Germany, the U.S.A. and other western countries have demonstrated that all democracies are endangered where the monetary re-distribution mechanism is allowed to proliferate. As time goes on, those who think that they live in democracies will live at best, in oligarchies or at worst, under fascist regimes. In medieval times, people thought they were badly off when they paid tithes: a tenth of their income or produce to the feudal landlord. In this respect, they were better off than we are nowadays. Today, more than one third of each DM or dollar goes to service capital. Those who gain most are the super rich, multinationals, big insurance companies and banks.

The question is whether we are finally willing to comprehend the social injustice that is caused by our present money system and change it or whether we wait until a major world-wide economic or ecological breakdown, war or social revolution occurs. As there is no way in which single individuals or small groups alone can change the monetary system, we must try to bring together those who understand how it can be changed with those who have the power to change it. It should be clear that:

- ■ there can be no accusation of those who, at present,

Distribution of Monetary Wealth in the F.R.G.

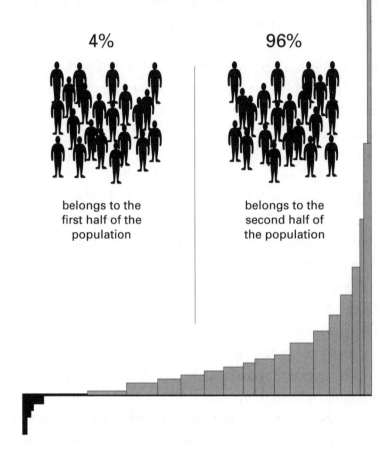

4%

belongs to the
first half of the
population

96%

belongs to the
second half of
the population

- To which half do you belong?
- How do these discrepancies develop?
- What are the consequences of this concentration?

FIGURE 11

profit from the interest system as this is totally within their legal rights;

■ what can be stopped, however, is the continual on-going extraction out of a given economy of money without work;

■ there should be no regulation as to where or how money may be invested in the future by those who have more than they need. If they are intelligent, they will keep it in the country anyway, which would create a new economic boom by abolishing the interest system.

THE POOR

Would the poor also benefit from a new money system? If resources were averaged, every German household in 1986 would have a private fortune of 90,000 DMarks. This would have been a splendid proof of our prosperity if it were evenly distributed. The ugly reality is that one half of the population owned 4% of that wealth and the other half, 96% (*Figure 11*). More exactly, the wealth of 10% of the population grows continually at the cost of all others.

This explains why, for instance, lower middle-class families in Germany increasingly seek financial support from social welfare agencies. Unemployment and poverty are growing in spite of a sizable welfare system set up to overcome both.

The largest factor in the redistribution of wealth is interest which transfers daily millions of DMarks from those who work to those who own capital. Although most governments try

Interest Rate vs. Unemployment
and Bankruptcies
A Tight Supply of Money Causes Interest Rates to Rise
Causing Rising Unemployment and Bankruptcies

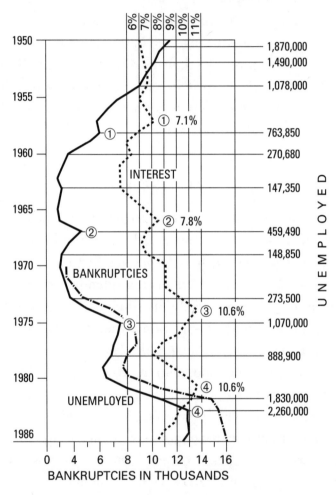

* Why do we lose jobs when interest rates are high?
* What causes these interdependencies?
* How can the situation be rectified?

FIGURE 12

to rectify the resulting imbalance through taxation, the result is nowhere near a balance. In addition, the costs of growing bureaucracies are affecting everybody through increased taxes. The human costs in terms of time and energy, plus the humiliation involved in getting through the "red tape," are seldom if ever taken into account.

The absurdity of a monetary system which robs people first of their fair share in the "free market economy" and then – through some of the most inefficient procedures imaginable – returns some of this money in the form of welfare payments to the same people, has rarely been exposed by the "experts" nor been discussed in public. As long as those 80% of the people who pay don't understand how they pay, could it be otherwise?

A practical comparison of rising interest rates and increasing bankruptcies in business and industry, as well as unemployment rates following with a time-lag of about two years (*Figure 12*) provides another compelling argument for the introduction of an interest-free monetary system. Also, social costs like alcoholism, families breaking up and increases in criminal behaviour are additional costs which are not taken into account in the above statistics but could be effectively reduced by the monetary reform.

If we look at the dilemma of Third World countries (*Figure 13*), we see our own situation through a magnifying glass. It is like a caricature of what happens in industrially developed countries, due to the same structural fault in the monetary system. However, the difference is that industrially developed countries as a whole, profit while the developing countries pay. Every day we receive $300 million in interest payments from Third World coun-

DEVELOPMENT AID

Every day, the Third World pays the Industrialized
World $300 million in interest!

- Our development aid is only half that amount!
- How long will this be possible?
- How can this exploitation be reduced?

FIGURE 13

tries: that is, twice the amount of the "development aid" which we give them.

Of the Third World countries' total debt of one trillion dollars in 1986, about one third was lent in order to repay interest on previous loans. There is no hope that these countries will ever be able to pull out of the situation without a major crisis or fundamental policy change. If war means hunger, starvation and death, social and human misery, we are right in the middle of the "Third World War" (*Figure 14*). It is an undeclared war. It is a war fought with usurious interest rates, manipulated prices and unfair trade conditions. It is a war which forces people into unemployment, sickness and criminal behaviour. Do we have to tolerate this indefinitely?

There is no doubt that those who are at present worse off in the monetary system we have created account for more than half of the world's population. The situation in the Third World would change momentarily if their debts were to be written off partially or totally by lender nations and banks. This is often advocated by progressive economists and, in fact, is already happening. However, unless the basic flaw in the money system is abolished, the next crisis is pre-programmed. Therefore, one of the important steps for a more stable economic system on a world-wide scale is to make known among those who would undoubtedly gain most – the poor and the developing countries – that an alternative system could be chosen.

WE ARE LIVING IN WORLD WAR III ALREADY

... an economic war. It is a non-declared war; a war of usurious interest rates, ruinous prices, and distorted exchange conditions ... Remote controlled interest rates and terms of trade have so far killed millions of people on a plundered planet. They are killed by hunger, sickness, unemployment and criminality.

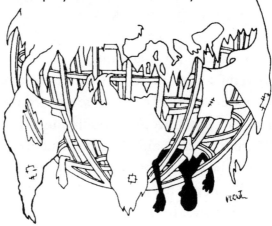

- Do we have to put wp with these conditions?
- Do revolutions present viable solutions?
- What are the real causes of war?

FIGURE 14

THE CHURCHES AND SPIRITUAL GROUPS

Many of the great political and religious leaders such as Moses, Jesus Christ, Mohammed, Luther, Zwingli and Gandhi have tried to reduce social injustice by prohibiting interest payments. They understood the cause of the problem. However, they did not come up with a practical solution, and thus, the basic flaw in the system remained unchanged. The prohibition of interest payments in the Christian world by the Popes during the Middle Ages in Europe, for instance, just shifted the problem to the Jews, who became, at that time, the leading bankers of Europe. While the Jews were not allowed to take interest from each other, they could do so from the Gentiles. In Islam, people do not pay interest for a loan, but the lending banks or individuals become shareholders in their business and take part of the ensuing profits. In some cases this may be better – in others worse – than paying interest.

Nowadays the Christian churches and charitable organizations exhaust their followers with calls for donations to alleviate the worst social problems in industrially developed and developing countries. This remains symptomatic treatment as long as the systemic fault in our monetary system continues.

What is needed instead is the dissemination of information and an open discussion about the effects of the present monetary system and the solution in terms of monetary reform.

In Latin America, for instance, the Catholic Church is split between the conservative top hierarchy tending towards the western model of capitalism and the progressive base which is oriented towards the communistic model. The historic opportunity now is to present an interest-free economy as a third type of solution which is to be found neither in communism nor in capitalism but transcends both. It would go farther in providing social justice than any aid program. It would create a stable economy and offer the churches significant assistance in their efforts to bring peace to this earth.

In spiritual terms everything we find in the outside world is a reflection of our own inner selves, our belief systems, our wishes and our thoughts. A transformation of the outer world, therefore, requires a transformation of the inner world. One without the other is not possible.

The proliferation of esoteric knowledge and skills in many parts of the world indicates a profound shift in consciousness of an increasingly larger number of people. Their work on inner change provides the basis for outer change. Without this work a peaceful transformation of the monetary system may be impossible. Therefore, a great responsibility rests with those who serve humanitarian goals and are aware of the practical possibilities of monetary reform as one aspect of global transformation.

BUSINESS AND INDUSTRY

In an interest and inflation free economy the prices of goods and services would be regulated, as in today's capitalist societies, by supply and demand. What would change, however, is the distortion of the "free market" by the interest mechanism.

On average, every workplace in the German industry

carries a debt load of DM70–80,000 (> $35–40,000). Interest alone makes up as much as 23% of the average labor costs[25] *(see Figure 15)*. To the share of interest on borrowed capital must be added the interest share on the firm's own capital. The latter orients itself along the same interest rate as the former. This is why debts increase about two to three times faster than the economic productivity of the country *(see Figure 5)*. The proportion is constantly getting worse for those who work and for those who want to start a business.

We are witnessing increasing concentration in the industrial sector. Small businesses and industrial firms are being bought up by larger ones and larger ones are being bought up by even larger ones, until one day almost everybody in the so-called "free market economies" may work for a multi-national corporation. This development receives its impetus from the so-called "economies of scale" and from automation of larger industrial firms, but also from the surplus money gained by these businesses on the money market. Siemens and Daimler-Benz in Germany, for instance, earn more money through investments in the capital market than in the production sector. In fact, they have been characterized in the German press as large banks with a production front.

In contrast, smaller and medium-sized firms in order to expand usually have to borrow money and, therefore, are trapped in the interest and compound interest system. They can not capitalize on the economies of scale, and they cannot capitalize on capital.

Up to now our economy depends on capital. The German industrial representative, Mr. Schleyer, once said

LABOR COSTS ARE HIGHER THAN JUST SALARIES

For each 100 DM of direct salaries paid out in 1985 ...

... industrial firms had to add another 23 DM in interest.

- Where do these additional costs originate?
- What are the consequences?
- Can we change the distribution?

FIGURE 15

fittingly: "Capital must be served!" But in the new monetary system capital would be designed to serve the needs of the economy. It would have to offer itself to avoid penalty, i.e., it must serve us!

FARMERS

Because of the devastating effects of interest on our agricultural system, farming provides a particularly good case for a new money system. Agriculture is an industry based on ecology. In general, ecological processes follow a natural growth curve (*Curve A in Figure 1*) Industrial processes must follow the exponential growth curve of interest and compound interest, at present (*Curve C in Figure 1*). Since nature cannot be made to increase like capital, the industrialization of agriculture has created threatening problems for our survival.

In the first phase of industrialization, farmers bought bigger and better machinery. Then bigger farmers bought up smaller farms to become even larger, with the help of government subsidies and tax incentives. Then the signs of sickness began to appear and multiply: the depletion and pollution of water supplies; fertile soils becoming like dried-out and compacted deserts; the loss of more than 50% of all species; the overproduction of special items which could only be sold with more government subsidies; hybrid produce which is tasteless and poisonous; total reliance on oil for transportation, artificial fertilizers, insecticides, pesticides; vanishing rain-forest to supply packaging materials for long hauls between the places of production, storage, processing, selling and consuming.

Hurrah! 2.5 Percent Growth Again!

2.5% growth
today is as
much as 9%
in the 1950s

- Where does the insane pressure for growth originate?
- How can we free ourselves from this pressure?
- Why are stable economies impossible in the present system?

FIGURE 16

While interest is only one factor contributing to this development, introduction of an interest-free money system would be of particular importance for this societal sector which secures our survival. Interest-free loans, combined with land and tax reforms (*see Chapter 2*), might allow a larger number of people than presently expected to return to the land. Together with new methods of sustainable agriculture, we may witness the evolution of a different lifestyle, combining work and leisure, hand and "brain" work, high and low technology, to serve a more holistic approach to individual, agricultural and social development.

ECOLOGISTS AND ARTISTS

When we talk about economic growth, measured in the percentage increase of the GNP and compared to previous years, we usually forget that this increase is related to a larger amount every year. Thus, 2.5% growth today is, in fact, four times as much as 2.5% growth during the 1950s (*Figure 16*).

Why politicians, industrialists and union leaders still call for measures to boost economic growth is easily explained: During phases of decreasing growth rates, the discrepancy between income from capital and labor or the redistribution of wealth from labor to capital becomes more severe. This means increasing social and ecological problems and economic and political tensions.

Continual economic growth, however, results in the depletion of natural resources. *That means, in the present monetary system, we have a choice between ecological or eco-*

nomic collapse. In addition, the concentration of money in the hands of fewer people and large multi-national corporations creates a constant pressure for large scale investments, e.g., atomic power plants, huge dams for hydroelectric power, and arms. From a purely economic angle, the U.S.A. and Europe are displaying politically contradictory behavior. Installing bigger and better weapons against Russia on the one hand, and sending butter, wheat and technological know-how to Russia on the other, made perfect economic sense: Military production is the only area where the "saturation" point can be postponed indefinitely as long as "the enemy" is equally able to develop faster and better weapons. Profits in the military sector are far greater than any profits made in the civilian sectors of our economy.

As long as every investment has to compete with the money-making power of money on the money market, most ecological investments, aimed at creating sustainable systems (i.e., stopping quantitative growth at an optimal level), will be difficult to implement on a larger scale. Today, people who have to borrow money for ecological investments usually lose – economically. If interest could be abolished they might at least break even, although the difference from other investments (e.g., in the arms business) would still remain the same.

Let us take an investment in solar collectors as an example. If we can expect only a 2% return on our money, it would be economically unwise to invest in this otherwise sensible, ecological technology for producing hot water, since our money in a bank might pay a 7% return.

A change in the monetary system would provide people

with a chance at least to break even if they invest in the maintenance and improvement of the biological basis of life. This would create a very different impetus for individuals and groups to engage themselves in conservation measures and ecologically sound technologies.

Even the volume of economic activities would be more easily adjusted to real needs. Since high capital returns in order to pay off interest would not be needed any more, the pressure on overproduction and overconsumption would be considerably reduced. Prices could be reduced by 30 to 50% which pays for highly capital intensive technology. In theory, people would need to work only half of the time in order to keep the same standard of living.

Within the new monetary system, quantitative growth would most likely be changed into qualitative growth. People would have a choice of leaving their new money in a savings account where it would keep its value, or investing it in glass, china, furniture, art work or a solidly built house, which would keep their respective values. They might well opt for those investments which would enrich their daily lives. However, the higher the quality demanded, the more it would be produced. Thus we could expect a total revolution of values, which would almost certainly effect cultural and environmental issues. Many investments in art and ecological technologies would be able to compete given a "stable" money and sustainable way of life, and pay without making large profits. Thus art and ecology would soon become "economically feasible."

WOMEN

Why do so few women operate in the money sphere? Whether on the stock market or within the banking world, this is still a man's realm and exceptions only seem to prove the rule. I have ascertained from a fairly long-standing experience with women's issues and women's projects that most women intuitively feel that there is something wrong with this money system, although, like men, they do not clearly know what is wrong.

Women's fierce fight for equality, which is also largely an economic issue, has made them resentful about processes that produce inequity, like the money game. Most women understand experientially that whatever somebody gains without work, i.e., through interest and compound interest, somebody else has to work for it. The latter (in many cases) will be female. Of that half of the population which owns only 4% of the total wealth (*Figure 11*), the majority are women.

Women overwhelmingly carry the load of the economic chaos and social misery caused by the present money system everywhere in the world. The introduction of a new money system which serves as a "technically improved barter system" may well change their lot dramatically. For this reason, I expect a high percentage of women to be among the main movers for a more equitable exchange medium. They understand what it means to be exploited. Following the conversion, they may well get involved in banking and investing to a much larger extent. This would happen because they would understand that it would be a life-enhancing rather than destructive system in which they would operate. Last but not least, this money system fits their concept of power much better.

Men are used to the hierarchical model of power with an almighty top and a powerless base. Whoever gets a chunk of the cake leaves less for the others. It's a win/lose situation.

Women more often experience power as an infinitely expandable concept. Whenever someone adds power to a group, the whole group becomes more powerful. It's a win-win situation.

A monetary system which expands with growing needs but stops when these needs have been met almost automatically creates a win-win situation for everybody in the long run. Even in the short run, in a crisis situation, which is what we are in right now.

What women will want most for themselves and their children is that, instead of another of the hard revolutionary transitions which have caused such an endless amount of human misery in the past, the change – if it could happen before the crash – would provide a soft evolutionary transition.

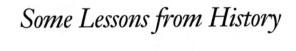

Some Lessons from History

CHAPTER FOUR

Some Lessons from History

THE MONETARY SYSTEM we have inherited is more than 2,000 years old. The German word for money, which is "Geld," links it rather precisely to its origin which was gold. Gold, a fairly useless metal except for jewelry and ornaments, became the preferred exchange medium around 700 B.C. in the Roman Empire. Money always meant coinage. This was the concept which was incorporated in the U.S. Constitution. Gold and silver coins (or their depository receipts) were the only fully legal tender in the U.S.A. until 1934. To this day, many people – mainly those who see the disadvantages of the practically unlimited possibilities for creating paper money – favor a return to the gold standard for money.

When Silvio Gesell published his book *Die Natürliche Wirtschaftsordnung* (*The Natural Economic Order*) in 1904, about three-quarters of the book dealt with this issue.[26] Against all the established economists of his time he tried to prove theoretically and with practical examples that the gold standard was not only unnecessary but detrimental to a well-functioning monetary system based on interest free money.

Today, we know that the gold standard is not a necessary precondition. There is no money system in the world now which is based on the gold standard. John Maynard Keynes, who was well acquainted with Silvio Gesell's work, helped to eliminate this barrier to a well-functioning economy in the 1930s. What he forgot to advocate, however, was the other essential ingredient: the replacement of interest by a circulation fee. This is largely why we are in trouble now and will be at regular intervals until we have learned the lesson.

In order to show how difficult a deep understanding of monetary issues really is, I would like to sketch out a few historic examples to illuminate this point.

BRAKTEATEN MONEY IN MEDIEVAL EUROPE

Between the 12th and the 15th century in Europe a money system was used called "Brakteaten." Issued by the respective towns, bishops and sovereigns, it not only helped the exchange of goods and services but also provided the means of collecting taxes. Every year the thin coins made from gold and silver were "recalled," one to three times re-minted and devalued on an average about 25% in the process.

Since nobody wanted to keep this money, people instead invested in furniture, solidly built houses, artwork and anything else that promised to keep or increase its value. During that time, some of the most beautiful sacred and profane works of art and architecture came into existence. "For while monied wealth could not accumulate, real wealth was created."[27]

We still think of this time as one of the cultural culmination points in European history. Craftsmen worked a five-day week, the "blue" Monday was introduced and the standard of living was high. In addition, there were hardly any feuds and wars between the various realms of power.

However, people obviously disliked the money which lost so much at regular intervals. Finally, towards the end of the 15th century, the "eternal" penny was introduced and with it came interest and accumulation of wealth in the hands of increasingly fewer people, as well as the accompanying social and economic problems. The lesson here is that taxes should be levied separately and not connected with the circulation fee on money.

THE WEIMAR REPUBLIC AND THE GOLD STANDARD

During the Weimar Republic (1924–33), the central bank's president, Hjalmat Schacht, had the desire to create an "honest" currency in Germany which – in his understanding meant a return to the gold standard. Since he could not buy enough gold on the world market adequate to the amount of money in circulation, he began to reduce the latter. The shorter supply of money resulted in rising interest rates, thereby reducing the incentives and possibilities for investment, forcing firms into bankruptcy, and increasing unemployment, which led to the growth of radicalism and finally helped Hitler to gain more and

Unemployment Impoverishes, Poverty Radicalizes

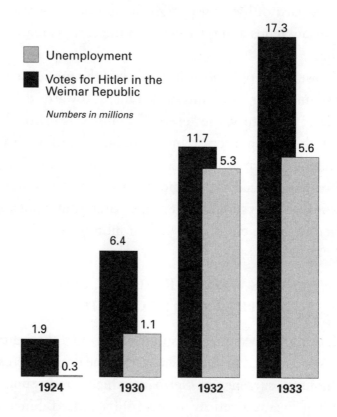

- Are we endangered by a new radicalism?
- What causes the "new poverty"?
- Can we prevent this development?

FIGURE 17

more power. *Figure 17* shows the links between growing poverty and radicalism in the Weimar Republic.

This development had been foreseen by Silvio Gesell – although for different reasons. Already in 1918, shortly after World War I, when everybody talked about peace and many international organizations were created to secure that peace, Gesell published the following warning in a letter to the editor of the newspaper *Zeitung am Mittag* in Berlin:

> In spite of the holy promise of all people to banish war, once and for all, in spite of the cry of millions 'Never a war again,' in spite of all the hopes for a better future, I have this to say: If the present monetary system, based on interest and compound interest, remains in operation, I dare to predict today, that it will take less than 25 years for us to have a new and even worse war. I can foresee the coming development clearly. The present degree of technological advancement will quickly result in a record performance of industry. The build-up of capital will be rapid in spite of the enormous losses during the war, and through its over-supply will lower the interest rate. Money will then be hoarded. Economic activities will diminish and increasing numbers of unemployed persons will roam the streets ... within the discontented masses, wild, revolutionary ideas will arise and also the poisonous plant called "Super-Nationalism" will proliferate. No country will understand the other, and the end can only be war again.[28]

Seen historically *after the facts*, money was made to be in short supply by the central bank and hoarded by private people. The effects were disastrous. Yet up to this day, central bankers seem to be ignorant of the fundamental cure for problems they face every day.

*Monetary Reform in the Context of
Global Transformation: An Example
of How to Make the Change*

CHAPTER FIVE

Monetary Reform in the Context of Global Transformation: An Example of How to Make the Change

T HE FACT THAT this book concentrates on the issue of monetary reform as one important aspect of the total global transformation which we are about to witness does not mean that it is more important than other aspects. From organizational to individual transformation, from technological to spiritual transformation, we need change.

Money, how it works and what it does to society, has been notoriously overlooked although it seems to be a fairly central piece of the puzzle. Neither experts nor those who occupy themselves with alternatives to the present economic system seem to worry much about this issue. It may not be more important but it certainly is not less important than others. It simply affects everybody.

REPLACING REVOLUTION WITH EVOLUTION

While the three reforms – in money, land and tax systems – proposed in this book constitute only a small part of the overall changes that are necessary for survival on this planet, they may fit readily into many attempts to create a new relationship between human beings and nature – and human beings and their fellow human beings. *Social justice, ecological survival and freedom are threatened where we allow the proliferation of societal structures which in themselves tend to work against these goals.*

The proposed reforms clearly combine the advantages of both capitalism and communism. They avoid their respective shortcomings and provide a "third type of solution." They would allow individual freedom and growth together with a free market system, and with a far greater degree of social equity. At the same time, they would stop the exploitation of the large majority by a small minority – without introducing the heavy regulations of a planned economy and an almighty bureaucracy.

The communist attempt to create freedom from exploitation failed because, in order to secure a minimum existence for everybody, communism eliminated personal freedom. The capitalist tendency, on the other hand, by letting land and capital be exploited in an unrestricted practice of personal freedom has endangered the minimum existence of the majority of people. Both systems have gone too far in their respective directions. One has set the priority of freedom from hunger above freedom to choose one's own life style. The other has set the top priority on personal freedom which, in the present monetary system, can only be achieved by very few people. Both are partially right, but both have failed to create the preconditions for a genuinely human existence including genuine freedom.

The reforms proposed here could reduce governmental intervention and create an ecological economy in which goods and services could be produced at an optimum size and level of complexity because that is where they would be the cheapest, i.e., most competitive in a free system.

While the full extent to which wealth is redistributed through the monetary and land systems is less obvious in highly industrialized countries, because of the exploitation of developing countries, the working people in the latter really pay the price for the monetary systems of the industrialized world. Although they suffer most, there is little hope that these ideas will be used first in the Third World where small elite groups dominate in terms of money, land and political power.

However, there may be a possibility for change in the smaller democratic nations of Europe. Scandinavia, for instance, with a majority of wealthy and well educated people, might prove comparatively well open to social change. And this is what monetary reform is all about.

At the U.N. World Commissions Public Hearing in Moscow on December 11, 1986, A. S. Timoschenko of the Institute of State and Law, U.S.S.R. Academy of Sciences, proposed that:

> "Today we cannot secure security for one state at the expense of the other. Security can only be universal, but security cannot only be political or military, it must be as well

CIRCULATION GUARANTEE

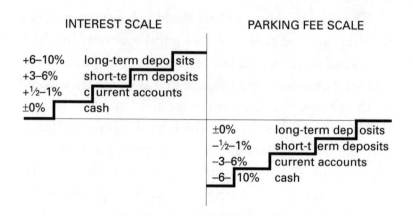

INTEREST SCALE   PARKING FEE SCALE

+6–10%   long-term deposits
+3–6%   short-term deposits
+½–1%   current accounts
±0%   cash

                            ±0%   long-term deposits
                            –½–1%   short-term deposits
                            –3–6%   current accounts
                            –6–10%   cash

AND
AVERAGE ANNUAL COST OF CREDIT

in the interest system (1991)

a.	Bank fees	1.7%
b.	Risk premium	0.8%
c.	Liquidity	3.0%
d.	Inflationary adjustments	4.0%
	Total	**9.5%**

in the neutral-money system

a.	Bank fees	1.7%
b.	Risk premium	0.8%
c.	Liquidity	0.0%
d.	Inflationary adjustments	0.0%
	Total	**2.5%**

FIGURE 18

ecological, economical and social. It must ensure the fulfill-
ment of the aspirations of humanity as a whole."[32]

The struggle of humankind for social and economic
justice has been long and fierce. It has created sharp di-
visions in political orientations and religious beliefs. It has
cost many lives. It is indeed urgent that we come to the
understanding that nobody can obtain security for one-
self at the expense of another, or at the expense of the
environment on which we depend. In order to make this
feasible we need some deep and practical changes in the
structures of our social framework. Hopefully the changes
proposed in this book will contribute to the creation of
security and justice for people and our global environment, and finally begin to replace revolution with evolution.

A POSSIBLE SOLUTION FOR THE NEAR FUTURE

Before the money system could be reformed, a large
section of the population must realize that we have to limit
money to its functions as an exchange medium, as a scale
for prices and as a constant standard of value. If this rec-
ognition is transformed into political action, then the
central bank, as directed by the government, would employ
a *parking fee* rather than interest to keep money in circulation.

THE PARKING FEE CREATES
A NEUTRAL MONEY SYSTEM

As a method to secure circulation, the *parking fee* would make possible all necessary transactions. If there is enough money available to accomplish all necessary transactions, then it is not necessary to put more into circulation. Hereby, the growth of the amount of money available follows the growth of the economy and this follows, once again, the natural growth curve (*curve in Figure 1*).

If somebody has more cash than they need, at any time, they pay it into their bank. Depending on the length of time the money is deposited, the parking fee will be either diminished or waived. *Figure 18* shows how today's interest scale would be replaced by a parking fee scale. In the case of long term deposits there would be no fee; cash would have the highest fee.

The hoarding of cash in the new system could be avoided much more easily than by gluing a stamp on the back of a banknote as was done in Wörgl. Several suggestions have been made: One is a lottery system. It would ensure the circulation of cash by the withdrawal of one specific note denomination, in the same way as a lottery draw.

Based on today's eight denominations (in the case of the German Mark DM 5/10/50/100/200/500/1000), e.g., the eight coloured balls representing different bank note denominations would be mixed with white balls representing no conversion in such a way that on statistical average – a conversion of one denomination would occur once or twice per year.

Draws could take place, for example, on the first Saturday of each month. Once a denomination is drawn, the conversion period could go on until the end of the month. The drawn notes would remain legal tender and could be used for payment in all shops. However, the respective fee would have to be deducted from payments with these bank notes.

Another option is to exchange the invalid notes against payment of the exchange fee at a bank or post office. Because no one likes to pay fees, everyone would limit their use of cash to the necessary amount, and surplus money would be paid into bank accounts.

The exchange would be facilitated by giving the new note denominations a new colour and size. New DM 100 yellow notes replace the old blue notes which go out of circulation. The concealment of overdue notes can be avoided by making the new notes slightly longer or wider so that every false note would jut out of a bundle, no matter how thick.

Unlike stickers, or stamp money, the drawing of denominations has the advantage that there is no need to print new money. We could keep the same money we have today and the actual cost of the system would be no higher than the replacement of worn out notes today.

In this new neutral money system, banks are under the same obligation as everybody else to pass the money on to those who need it. If they have interest free deposits on their books, and don't lend the money out or transfer it to the central or regional bank, they would also have to pay the parking fee. People receiving a credit would pay no interest but banking charges and risk premiums, comparable to those included in every bank loan. The two amount to about 2.5% (1991 in Germany) of the average credit costs (*see Figure 18*). In Switzerland, they only amounted to about 1.5% of the average credit costs. In industrially developing countries, they were even two to three times as high.

*What Can I Do to Help
in the Transition Period?*

CHAPTER SIX

What Can I Do to Help in the Transition Period?

T HE GREATEST OBSTACLE to the transformation of the monetary system is that few people understand the problem and even fewer know that there is a solution. However, since October 1987, when $1.5 trillion vanished on Wall Street, people are more interested in listening. To be informed exactly about the way in which interest and compound interest works is the first step towards change. To be able to discuss the solution and its varied implications is the next step.

BE INFORMED, INCREASE THE AWARENESS OF OTHERS

Start among friends and family members to experience how far you can explain the issue. Then move on to people you know less well and finally don't hesitate to talk to your banker, insurance broker, local politician, journalists and media people. Many discussions with professionals, bankers and economists have convinced me that there are no "real" difficulties, except the mental blocks created by education and limiting belief systems about what money is and how it should function.

Be aware that money is one of the central issues in many people's lives. Therefore, it is linked strongly with people's perception of themselves and the world. Generosity or greed, openness or isolation, warmth or coldness – how people behave in other areas will be reflected in their attitude towards money. Usually it is difficult to treat money as a separate issue. However, you have to explain the way in which interest accumulates wealth before you deal with the symptoms which appear, e.g., in the social and political arena. Otherwise, the whole discussion may become more difficult.

Be aware that monetary reform, although it is linked to many other problems, is not going to cure all of them automatically. It will not by itself provide for the poor, the old, the sick or for other social needs. Monetary reform will make it easier to help these groups. But that does not mean that we can do without special programs or mechanisms to solve other social problems. The same applies to ecology, conservation and other tasks.

Just following what happens in the world through the media any day will increase your understanding of the urgency and feasibility of this change and the responsibility which everybody who knows of a solution carries in respect to making it more widely known.

SPONSOR MODEL EXPERIMENTS

The most important precondition for an interest-free monetary system is to set up some "real life examples" which will give us an idea about the effects this change may have on a larger scale.

Preferably, the regions or countries interested in a trial run should coordinate their action in order to achieve a greater validity in observing the results under different social, cultural and economic conditions. The areas selected should be large enough to provide relevant results for the whole country. A high level of autonomy would be desirable. That means that many of the goods and services needed should be available in the area where the experiment happens.

The other possibility is to choose a region which is depressed – usually because of lack of diversification – and create an impetus for a more differentiated and stable economy through the introduction of a new monetary system. The latter case may be the more tempting because where a situation is bad enough people tend to be more open to change, mainly when they see – as in the case of Wörgl (*Chapter 2*) – that they have everything to gain and nothing to lose in the process. On the other hand, a relatively active, diversified and economically healthy area may also see advantages in the introduction of a new monetary system very clearly and here the success of the change may be evident faster.

It would create more validity not to limit experiments to one or the other situation exclusively, in order to find out what interest-free money means in different social contexts.

START A LOCAL EXCHANGE
TRADING SYSTEM

Of all the attempts to exchange goods and services outside the present money systems, the one Michael Linton has started on Vancouver Island, Canada, is the most easily adaptable to any locality and, therefore, the best known world-wide.

The LET (Local Exchange Trading) System operates quite simply as a system of accounts of "green" dollars, without a fee on the money, but a small fee on each transaction. People arrange among themselves how many "green" and how many "normal" dollars each item they sell or buy will cost. They pass on their credits and debits to a computerized accounting center. Their limits to go into debt can be determined, at the outset, and changed when necessary later, in order to minimize the risk for all participants. Obviously, the more people participate, the more rewarding the system will be.

In this way, a small community near Vancouver helped a dentist who was young and had no money to build up a practice. The community built a house and surgery, largely from green dollars. The dentist then treated people for a certain percentage of green dollars.

The LET Systems work well in the beginning but in some instances there have been problems or collapse[29] where large surpluses or deficits occurred. In part this is because with no circulation fee there is no incentive to recycle money.

However, it still makes sense to support experiments with different types of circulation systems than the one we have at present, in order to enable people to understand the functions and purposes of money better. Practical examples provide a better learning experience than any book or lecture.

SUPPORT ETHICAL INVESTMENT

One immediate step everybody can take toward transition is to see to it that their own surplus money gets invested in an ethical way. As more and more people begin to realize its social and moral implications, ethical investment in the U.S.A. has mushroomed into a multi-million dollar movement. In the words of Hazel Henderson, "a growing army of common folk have stood on their doorsteps, smelt the rot and can no longer let what they do with their money counteract with what they do with their lives."[30]

Ethical investors look at their potential investments in economic and social terms. People like Robert Schwartz, an early pioneer in socially responsible investment, started by eliminating from their list of possible investments the companies that were major defense suppliers or had unfair labor policies, polluters, including nuclear utilities, that were destructive to the environment and those firms who made their assets available to repressive government regimes like South Africa.[31]

Environmental awareness is not only a vital moral standpoint but in many cases also makes good money sense, mainly when the situation is bad enough through the previously ruthless exploitation of resources. The nuclear power industry, for instance, with its accidents and cleanup costs has proven to be a bad lemon for investors in the U.S.A., whilst alternative energy has done well lately.

The greatest advantage of an ethical investment policy is that it can be put into practice right now. Whether we change the monetary system sooner or later, ethical investment is a splendid idea in any money system.

Practical Cases Today
Embryos of a New Economy

CHAPTER SEVEN

Practical Cases Today
Embryos of a New Economy

THERE ARE TWO major obstacles preventing the practical conversion of our interest-based money into a means of exchange which would serve everyone. First: Few people seem to understand the problem, and secondly, successful experiments are thinly spread all over the world in comparison to "normal" money trade.

Taken as a group though, these experiments are not only encouraging evidence that everyone can do something immediately, but they also provide us with a picture of what a transformation from the "bottom up" would look like. If enough people understood what issues are at stake, it would be possible to change our money system without state support. The models we are about to discuss differ in function – savings and loans on the one side, and exchange of goods and services on the other – as well as in their scope from local to nation-wide.

At a local level, the Canadian LET System offers an interest free means of exchange for groups, communities, villages or suburbs with a minimum of 20 and a maximum of 5,000 members.

The Swiss WIR-Wirtschaftsring (Economic Cooperative) shows how a practically interest-free accounting system for the exchange of goods and services can bring significant advantages to small and middle sized firms.

The Danish and Swedish JAK systems provide countrywide interest-free savings and loans schemes under conditions significantly better than those available from commercial banks.

Taken together these models prove that an interest-free money system which fulfills exactly the same functions as an interest based money system is practically possible. It proves that those who use it can benefit from such systems otherwise they would not continue to exist.

THE LET SYSTEM

In every village, every city and every region there are people with abilities and resources which are not used in the established economic system, yet there is a demand for such abilities and resources. An exchange network which advertises through billboards, newspapers, data banks, radio, or other means, gives people the chance to share these skills with one another, and enrich the life of the community in the real sense of the word, without using the established money system.

Of all exchange models LETS is the most widely used. There are hundreds of LET Systems in the U.S.A., Australia, Europe, New Zealand and many other countries. The first was established by Michael Linton in January,

1983, in Comox Valley, Vancouver Island, British Columbia, Canada. In 1990 the organization had around 600 members with a yearly turnover of $325,000 "green" dollars. These green dollars are the unit of payment for LETS, and are equal in value to the normal Canadian dollar.

Whatever a person may be prepared to pay for a task or piece of work is credited to the account of the one who performs the task and debited to the account of the person who buys the service. Interest is not paid for either credits or debits. Since the value of the normal clearing unit – the green dollar is equal to the Canadian dollar, inflation works as a circulation control since unused credits devalue at the rate of inflation. Because everyone is responsible for the cooperative debts, namely for unpaid debts, it is important that people know each other and learn to trust each other.

Limiting a LET System to a locality makes sense at the start of a program until more people learn to come to terms with the responsibility the system demands. Unfortunately it has not been possible to pay taxes in green dollars. If such payments were made possible then the local municipality or county would become partner of the LET System and would be able to finance investments in green dollars.

The advantages are obvious: Local people grow richer and the state or municipality gets access to an incredibly inexpensive work creation program.

Legally LETS does not impinge upon the established legal system in most countries, neither does it go against the monopoly of the state to print money, because it is no more than a local barter club or bookkeeping system.

LETS fills a gap in the market left by an economic system which is always in search of the cheapest production location, destroying in the process the local autonomous economic structure. It is true that the free world market offers benefits and that it has contributed to the prosperity we enjoy today in many parts of the world. However, it is also true that this prosperity has been created at the expense of workers in the so-called "low-wage countries," at the expense of non-renewable energy sources and the stability of regional economic structures.

It is important, therefore, to renew the local and regional economy. The economic ups and downs of the world market can be counteracted only if the internal economy of a region or a locality acts as a stable complementary system in balance with the global exchange of goods. The stronger the entire economic system, the stronger its individual elements can be.

In this respect, LETS is a locally based answer to the power of large corporations and state monopoly systems who have become highly problematic for small political and economic structures. The LET System is immune from local or international recessions, interest on debts, thefts and money shortages. The world money system can collapse; the dollar or DM can lose their value; unemployment may rise, but the green dollar still functions because it is guaranteed one hundred percent by work and by goods, and only functions if people cooperate in a direct exchange. Its main strength is that it cannot be used for the purpose of speculation, or one-sided enrichment.

The advantage of LETS is that it is limited only by

the time and energy a person is prepared to invest. These features can be decisive criteria for the introduction and extensive application of LETS, when interests are high and money is in short supply. Experience has shown that the people who are excluded from the normal economic system turn out to bring unusual talents when they join the LET System. Part-time occupations and hourly-rate jobs ranging from baby sitting, nursery and garden work, window cleaning, fruit preserving, to spring cleaning are some examples of LETS exchanges.

At first, LETS met with significant opposition. Leftists thought it was a plot of the right, and to the right it sounded like a communist takeover. Some business people thought it was a trick to take money from them. Men appeared more suspicious of the proposal, but women were significantly more pragmatic. "We should see if it works for us, and if it does, then why not use it?" Most members were fascinated because the system is easy to use, and because it has a self regulatory growth potential which is dependent on the number of transactions the system can absorb.

LETS can be combined with the existing money system quite easily. The origin of green dollars is totally decentralized and is related from its root level to the creativity of those who earn it. Because green dollars cannot leave the local area to buy Japanese cars or dresses from Hong Kong, every commercial transaction encourages the development of local resources. An unemployed mother in Courtney expressed her satisfaction this way: "… it gives me the feeling I am doing something for the community, because every time I buy something with green dollars,

I know I am helping someone improve their financial situation."

THE WIR NETWORK
AND SIMILAR ASSOCIATIONS

Switzerland has had a country-wide exchange network since 1934 whose goal is to provide enterprises with reasonable credits and to help its members to get higher turnovers and profits. The WIR (pronounced *vir* – short for *Wirtschaft* = economy in German) was founded by sympathizers of the Free Money System, the so-called *"Freiwirte"* (Free Economists). As an exchange ring the WIR works on the same basis as the LET System and similar to barter clubs: a cashless accounting system is run by a central office, cash withdrawals of deposits are not allowed and, therefore' credits can be interest free.

In 1990 WIR had about 53,730 members, 16,788 official accounts and a half yearly turnover of about 0.8 billion WIR, as the unit is called. The WIR, as a unit of payment, has the same value as the Swiss Franc. Because WIR money needs information to function in order to connect up supply and demand, the administrative group publishes a monthly magazine as well as three catalogues per year, showing products and services offered within the system.

The WIR defines itself quite openly as a support system for middle-sized business in competition with stronger and larger enterprises, helping those companies to fight an ever larger and intervening government. The organization is structured like a bank, and has its main office in Basel, seven regional offices throughout Switzerland with a total staff of one hundred and ten employees. Payments are made with forms not unlike normal bank cheques, with credit cards and bank forms. All transactions are either credited or debited by the central office. Savings do not accrue interest, and loans are charged only a minimal fee. Money is "created" in that a transaction takes place, exactly as described for the LET System. The difference here is that it is a nation-wide system and that it is limited to business. In 1990 the costs of the WIR organization were covered by a quarterly membership fee of eight Swiss Franks or 32 SFr per year, plus costs of 0.6–0.8% for every transaction.

In spite of an almost 60-year success in Switzerland the cooperative barter system has not been repeated in any other country in Europe. There are several reasons for this. In Germany in 1934, after countless "clearing houses," "clearing societies" and "exchange banks," organized basically on WIR Ring principles, had attracted many ordinary people, a commission of inquiry under the chairmanship of Mr. Schacht (then president of the German Central Bank) dictated legislation against the "misuse" of cashless payment systems in 1934. Paragraph 3 of this legislation spells out that cash withdrawals must be possible from any accounting system. This hit the core of the exchange rings. After this legal defeat and in spite of so many difficulties, no one expected that a commercial barter club would establish itself in Frankfurt/Main, the main banking centre of the German Federal Republic. The "Barter Clearing and Information" (BCI) group, although far more expensive in its services than the WIR Ring, has been successful. Instead of a 32 SFr (approx.

US $18) annual fee, the BCI charges DM 480 (approx. US $300) the first year. Unlike the 0.6 to 0.8% per transactions that the WIR Ring calculates, the BCI charge 1 to 2% per transaction.

The BCI is not considered a bank by the German Federal Supervisory Board because it only deals with goods and the exchange of services, and uses money only to calculate the value of the transactions. Its turnover in 1990 was DM 102,000,000 of which 30 million were barter fees. In contrast to WIR, the BCI has a consulting department to advise customers, and makes sure that companies do not carry negative balances for too long. After twelve months, accounts which show a minus have to be balanced. This allows those who have accumulated a positive balance and want to leave the system, the possibility of a compensation in German Marks after a period of six months and only if they leave the system. This feature overcomes the cash convertibility problem of the German credit laws, the problems of non-convertibility of the Swiss WIR currency into Swiss Francs, and the problems with members who do not want to be part of the system any more but cannot get out because they have high deposits, having provided services and goods for others in the system.

THE J.A.K. COOPERATIVE BANKS IN SWEDEN

The initials J.A.K. stand in Danish for land (*jord*), work (*arbete*) and capital (*kapital*), a movement which started in Denmark during the 1930s. At that time, most Danish farmers were heavily in debt and although their farms were productive, they could not hold on to their properties. Together with traders and producers, the farmers developed their own interest-free currency and banking system. Soon, it was clear to them that the new system could make their farms profitable again. Fearful that this example would become widespread, the Danish government prohibited the new currency from 1934 to 1938.

Today, the Danish and Swedish schemes (which started anew in the 1960s and 1970s) are basically similar and offer the same lending advantages, but they have different organizational methods. In Denmark, there are small JAK banks which offer standard services. In Sweden, the scheme operates through the postal banking service.

The long term socio-political aim of the Swedish JAK cooperative is to make interest unnecessary so that an economy can exist in balance with nature, without inflation or unemployment. Members are distributed all over the country. Early in 1991, the Swedish JAK group had 3,900 members and a total turnover of 34 million Swedish Crowns (about US $15 million). Already in 1993, the membership had risen to 38,000 and the turnover to 600 million Swedish Crowns (SEK). Since everyone saves, at least as much as they borrow, it is obvious that the total system maintains a constant balance.

Figures 19 and *20* show two examples of loans with different amounts, comparing bank loans with JAK loans over the same period of time.[33] Obviously everyone is better off when reciprocal saving and lending actually works without interest. Participation in the J.A.K. system, up to the total amount of a loan, makes unquestionable sense. Some people save above that commitment voluntarily, giving those who need a loan the opportunity to borrow before they save. People who only want to save, however, lose (through inflation) and, therefore, seldom participate.

The two examples depicted on pages 125 and 126 show a small short-term loan and a larger, long-term loan. All amounts are in Swedish Crowns (SEK).

EXAMPLE 1: A SEK 17,000 loan over three years, at 3.4% effective cost, is still significantly cheaper than an identical bank loan at 16.1%.

EXAMPLE 2: A larger credit, however, SEK 399,640 would cost 1.7% over 20 years, compared to an average bank loan costs of 13.1%.

In both cases, borrowers have not only the better conditions but additionally, a respectable savings of about 60% of the loan at the end of the established loan maturity.

In January 1990, the Ministry for Islamic affairs in Kuwait confirmed that the principle of the JAK system was compatible with Islamic economic principles. Since then, a substantial proportion of the JAK membership comes from the Arab world.

From a legal point of view, the JAK system is possible in Sweden because a registered association is allowed to keep and administer deposits and transactions.

ADVANTAGES AND DISADVANTAGES OF ALTERNATIVE MONEY AND CREDIT SYSTEMS

Exchange rings, barter clubs, and savings and loan associations are embryos of a new economy because they offer advantages to their members, otherwise no one would use them. Goods and services worth US $2 billion are bar-

Comparison Between Loans in the J.A.K. Systems and the Normal Bank, Example 1

	JAK	Bank
Amount saved monthly in SEK	500	500
Savings period in months	12	12
Total amount saved in SEK	6,000	6,000
Interest earned (10% bank) in SEK	0	325
Less tax in SEK	0	−97
Accessible funds in SEK	6,000	6,228
Loan amount in SEK	12,000	11,336
Loan costs deducted at disbursement	−636	−200
Amounts available in SEK	17,364	17,364
Interest (14% bank) in SEK	0	2,741
Net costs after deductions in SEK	445	1,191
Service charges, organization in SEK	0	380
Total costs in SEK	445	2,299
Effective loan rate of interest % p.a.	3.4	16.1
Quarterly installments in SEK	1,000	776–1,133*
Savings during repayment in SEK	834	0
Quarterly payments in SEK	1,834	1,188
(611.33 SEK monthly with JAK)		
Quarterly payments after tax deduction (average)	1,818	1,120
Repayment period in months	36	36
Payment to borrower 39 months after loan disbursement in SEK (12 ¥ 834 SEK with JAK)	10,008	0

*Amortization payment varies during the period of amortization for an installment credit.
Source: Per Almgren, "J.A.K. – An Interest-Free Savings and Loan Association in Sweden," Tumba, 1990.*

FIGURE 19

Comparison Between Loans in the J.A.K. Systems and the Normal Bank, Example 2

	JAK	Bank
Amount saved monthly in SEK	2,000	2,000
Savings period in months	72	72
Total amount saved in SEK	144,000	144,000
Interest earned (10% bank) in SEK	0	48,840
Less tax in SEK	0	−14,651
Accessible funds in SEK	144,000	178,189
Loan amound in SEK	308,000	221,651
Loan costs deducted at disbursement	−52,360	−200
Amounts available in SEK	399,640	399,640
Interest (13% bank) in SEK	0	465,319
Net costs after deductions in SEK	36,652	327,273
Service charges, organization in SEK	0	1,550
Total costs in SEK	36,652	327,273
Effective loan rate of interest % p.a.	1.7	13.1
Quarterly installments in SEK	3,423	429–7,133*
Savings during repayment in SEK	2,995	0
Quarterly payments in SEK	6,418	7,648
(2,139.33 SEK monthly with JAK)		
Quarterly payments after tax deduction (average)	6,011	6,114
Repayment period in months	270	270
Payment to borrower 273 months after loan disbursement in SEK (90 ¥ 2,995 SEK with JAK)	269,550	0

*Amortization payment varies during the period of amortization for an installment credit.
Summary: JAK financing gives lower total costs, often lower or equally large monthly payments, and more left over afterwards.*

FIGURE 20

tered yearly in the U.S.A. Taking into account the growing number of transactions, based on barter, between Eastern and Western Europe, as well as industrialized and developing countries, it is estimated that between 10 to 30% of the world trade is barter trade. Everywhere barter trade allows an additional volume of trade which would not be possible within the normal monetary system. The basic features of all exchange or barter systems are very similar:

- Members hold an account in a central office.
- Accounts are held in fictive clearing units (green dollars, WIR, etc.) and their value is identical to the national currency.
- An overdraft up to a particular limit is allowed, and members with positive balance become *de facto* lenders.
- Positive credit balances receive no interest, loans are interest-free, or (compared to market interest) carry very low interest.
- Cash deposits are sometimes allowed, and cash withdrawals are basically not allowed, or are limited.
- Members inform the central office about all transactions by telephone, in writing, or through electronic mail.
- The central office administers all settlements.
- The central office is paid by either yearly contributions and/or a fee per transaction by buyer and/or seller.
- The participants determine the price of the clearing unit themselves.

- The central office can demand a reserve to cover a loan against losses, and for cases of misuse.
- The central office is responsible for coordinating and informing members of credit and lending needs.

Needless to say, barter and exchange systems, specializing at a local, national or international level, have benefited greatly from the new information technology. The notion of a free exchange of goods and services as envisaged by Gesell and Proudhon, is now much easier to implement where information travels fast to any place in the world.

It is important to understand that barter clubs reverse today's banking principles. They reward those who exchange goods and services with interest free money and punish those who sit on their surplus money. It does not pay to keep green dollars or WIR sitting on an account, since there is no interest to be gained. If the group who uses the barter system is closely representative of the total market, then this economic microcosm will function well. An economy which would consist of a hundred decentralized barter clubs would have to pay only the costs for clearing and information, instead of the heavy load of interest.

Experience shows that excessive lending, i.e., long-standing negative accounts, can be just as dangerous as a high saving rate, i.e., long-standing positive accounts. To prevent the first from occurring, a deadline can be used to urge people to balance the extreme negative accounts, stipulating, for example, that negative balances have to be paid in the normal currency after one year, to be paid into a trust account, until a positive balance has been achieved.

To prevent the second from occurring, a parking fee would be introduced to encourage people to part with their savings. Many exchange ring systems tend towards stagnation because too many members save too much. The LET System in Comox Valley and other localities grew to a point and then stagnated suddenly when the possibility for meaningful investment disappeared. However, economic activities would liven up the moment credit becomes available to members.

Therefore, the exchange should be linked to a banking service. To simplify bank procedures for those with a large credit surplus, and to make negotiations for credit seekers easier, it would be possible to establish credits in green dollars (or the respective unit of barter). Large risks would have to be correspondingly assessed and covered by risk premiums and brought into balance with a positive credit balance.

The reward for the individual who saves would be no extra money or interest – but rather the possibility to keep his or her money without loss on a savings account. In that respect, a parking fee as circulation incentive provides the system with an impetus similar to interest. What disappears are the multiple credit back payments and, with them, both the unhealthy growth of the economic system and the interest-based one-sided advantages for money lenders as we know them today.

Two important problems need to be mentioned:
(1) The first is tax evasion. This was a prevalent problem among the commercial barter clubs in the

U.S.A. some years ago. As a result legislation has been passed in Washington, D.C. allowing tax officials to look into the accounts of all members of a barter club.

(2)   This leads to the second problem, namely that of the right to privacy. A perfect central accounting system would not only be an ideal instrument for economic transactions without the heavy load of interest, but also an ideal supervisory system for a totalitarian government. Such a perfect quantitative and qualitative information service has been the dream of societal planners in both East and West. Already in 1897, Solvay suggested a cashless economy, based on centralized accounts, which would register every movement in people's lives, and actually draw a diagram of their activities, and of everyone's actual relationships. In the 19th century, it was technically impossible to deal with the amounts of information necessary for such a scheme, but (as everyone knows) the situation has changed drastically in the last few decades.

A cashless money system carries the implicit possibility of checking up on the diagram of everybody's activities through the records of all transactions from their bank accounts. We should be conscious that a state monopoly, combined with a totally cashless monetary system, could become very dangerous, indeed, for our personal freedom.

In summary, I would like to restate my proposal:

The combination of an exchange ring, like the LET System or WIR exchange ring – with a savings and loans association, like the JAK System – but based on a parking fee or circulation incentive to help all necessary transactions does not exist today, although it would be quite easy to bring into existence by linking together the long-standing practical experience with these two systems. Thus an interest-free money system would be created which would provide all the possibilities covered by the normal money system:

(1) Exchange
(2) Lending
(3) Saving

Different attempts with alternative money systems are politically meaningful, because they help us to understand how money works and the purpose money serves in our life. Practical experiences are important, because they encourage people to make changes on a wider basis. However, so far none of these attempts have changed the major problems caused by today's money system in the world economy. Therefore, the aim to introduce fundamental monetary change at a national and international level should be among our highest political priorities for a just world.

References

1. Eckhard Eilers, (unpublished manuscript) Rastede, 1985

2. Eilers, *ibid*.

3. Spiegel Interview: "Ich sehe die Risiken ganz ganau," talking about the danger of a financial crash and the debt-crisis, *Spiegel, No. 25,* Rudolf Augstein Co., Hamburg, 1987, p. 59

4. Helmut Creutz, *Wachstum bis zur Krise*, Basis Verlag, Berlin, 1986, p. 8

5. Dieter Suhr, *Geld ohne Merwert*, Knapp Verlag, Frankfurt/Main, 1983

6. Silvio Gesell, *Die Natürliche Wirtschaftsordnung*, Rudolf Zitzmann Verlag, Nuremberg, 1904, (IXth edition, 1949)

7. Werner Onken, "Ein vernessenes Kapital der Wirtschafts-geschichte. Schwanenkirchen, Wörgl und andere Freigeld-experimente," *Zeitschrift für Sozialökonomie*, Nr. 58/59, Mai 1983, pp. 3–20

8. Fritz Schwartz, *Das Experiment, von Wörgl*, Genossenschaft Verlag, Bern, 1952

9. Dietr Suhr, *Capitalism at its Best*, (unpublished manuscript), 1988, p. 122

10. Hans R. L. Cohrssen, "The Stamp Scrip Movement in the U.S.A." in *ibid,*, p. 118

11. *ibid.*, p. 122

12. Yoshito Otani, *Ursprung und Lösung des Geldproblems*, Arrow Verlag Gesima Vogel, Hamburg, 1981

13. Henry George, *Progress and Poverty*, San Francisco, 1879

14. Gesell, *op. cit.*, p. 74

15. Yoshito Otani, *Die Bodenfrage und ihre Lösung*, Arrow Verlag Gesima Vogel, Hamburg, 1981

16. Pierre Fornallaz, *Die Ökologische Wirtschaft*, AT Verlag, Stuttgart, 1986

17. Hermann Laistner, Die *Ökologische Wirtschaft*, Verlag Max Huber, Ismanning near Munich, 1986

18. John L. King, *On The Brink of Great Depression II, Future Economic Trends*, Goleta, CA, 1987, p. 36

19. Fritjof Capra, *The Turning Point*, Simon and Schuster, New York, 1982

20. UN World Commission on Environment and Development, *Our Common Future*, Oxford University Press, Oxford and New York, 1987, p. 294

21. Spiegel Interview, *op. cit.*, p. 59

22. John Maynard Keynes, *The General Theory of Employment, Interest and Money*, London, 1936, (reprinted 1967), p. 355

23. John L. King, *op. cit.*, p. 162

24. Aachener Nachrichten, 29.5.85

25. *Weltwirtschaftswoche*, Nr. 4, 1984, p. 23

26. Gesell, *op. cit.*

27. Hans R. L. Cohrssen, "Fragile Money" in *The New Outlook*, Sept. 1933, p. 40

28. *Zeitung am Mittag*, Berlin, 1918

29. Letter from Hendric de Ilde, Vancouver Island, Canada to David Weston, Oxford, UK, January 20, 1988

30. Hazel Henderson, quoted in Jennifer Fletcher, "Ethical Investment" in *International Permaculture Journal*, Permaculture International Ltd., Sydney, Australia, 1988, p. 38

31. Robert Schwartz, quoted in *ibid.*, p. 39

32. A. S. Timoschenko, quoted in UN World Commission on Environment and Development, *op. cit.*, p. 294

33. Per Almgren, *J.A.K.—An Interest-free Savings and Loan Assocaatitions in Sweden, Tumba*, 1990

Useful Addresses

AUSTRALIA
    LET System
    1 Ross Road
    Channon via Lismore
    NSW 2480

AUSTRIA
    Intl Assn for a Natural Economic Order
    Wallseerstrasse 45
    A4020 Linz

CANADA
    Landsman Community Services, Ltd.
    1600 Embleton Crescent
    Courtenay, B.C. V9N 6N8

DENMARK
    Folkesparekassen (JAK Bank)
    Herningvej 37
    DK 8600 Silkeborg

    JAK Natl Assn for Land, Work & Capital
    Drejegaardavej 4
    DK 8600 Silkeborg

GERMANY

Hamburger Geld und Bodenrechtsschule e.V.
Ringheide 24c
D 21149 Hamburg

Trion Institute
Gerberstr 9
D 22767 Hamburg

INDIA

Self Transformation Network for a Just World
35 CCI Chambers
Bombay 400 020

MEXICO

Intl Assn for a Natural Economic Order
902 Esquina Ruben Dario
Colina, Col. 28010

NEW ZEALAND

New Zealand Social Credit Institute
P. O. Box 910
Hamilton 2015

SRI LANKA

Center for Society and Religion
281 Dean's Road
Maradana, Colombo 10

SWEDEN

JAK Interest Free Economy
Vasagatan 14
S 54150 Skovde

SWITZERLAND ...

Intl Assn for a Natural Economic Order
Postfach 3359
CH 5001 Aarau

Talent-Experiment
Postfach 3062
CH 5001 Aarau

... SWITZERLAND
WIR
Auberg 1
CH 4002 Basel

UNITED KINGDOM
Intl Assn for a Natural Economic Order
Exeleigh South Starcross
Devon EXP 8PD

LETS LINK
61 Woodcock Road
Warminster, Wiltshire

New Economics Foundation
Universal House, 2nd Floor
88-94 Wentworth St.
London

U.S.A.
E. F. Schumacher Society
Box 76, RD 3
Great Barrington, Massachusetts 01230

Ithaca Money
P.O. Box 6578
Ithaca, New York 14851

Self Transformation Network for a Just World
2601 Cochise Lane
Okemos, Michigan 48864

Time Dollars
P.O. Box 19405
Washington, DC 20036

Journals

Der dritte Weg
Zeitschrift für die Natürliche Wirtschaftsordnung
Erftstrasse 57
D 45219 Essen
Germany

Dollars & Sense
One Summer St.
Sommerville, Massachusetts 02143
U.S.A.

Evolution
P.O. Box 3062
CH 5001 Aarau
Switzerland

Fragen der Freiheit
Badstrasse 35
D 73087 Boll
Germany

Permaculture Magazine
P. O. Box 1
Buckfastleigh, Devon TQ1 0LH
England

Index

ABOUT THIS BOOK

Dr. Margrit Kennedy wrote *Interest and Inflation Free Money* after ten years of research. She discovered it is virtually impossible to carry out sound ecological concepts without fundamentally altering the present monetary system based on interest.

She shows in this book how we can successfully eliminate interest and maintain sustainable economic development leading to a peaceful world that provides social equity in both industrialized and developing countries.

In this revised and expanded second edition, she discusses many experiments that have already demonstrated the wisdom of doing away with interest altogether.

Dr. Kennedy's simple and lucid writing style makes difficult concepts about money easy to understand. Anybody who cares where our world is headed must read this revolutionary book.

"It is possible to have a truly sustainable economic system which can prevent a global economic disaster and social chaos for billions of people in the world if we choose the soft evolutionary path of monetary change." —DR. MARGRIT KENNEDY

ABOUT THE AUTHOR

Margrit Kennedy is an architect, urban planner and Professor of Ecological Building Techniques at the University of Hannover in Germany.

Co-author Declan Kennedy is the initiatior and country coordinator of Global Action Plan for the Earth (GAP) and a member of the International board of GAP. He is also Margrit Kennedy's husband.

Margrit and Declan Kennedy have set up an Eco Village Project with a group of people in Steyerberg, Germany. This is one of the first European experiments in perma-culture.

Margrit has written several books and articles on woman and architecture, permaculture, and urban ecology.